access to

The SIXTEENTH-CENTURY REFORMATION

Geoffrey Woodward

THE HIGHFIELD SCHOOL
HIGHFIELD
LETCHWORTH
HERTS SG6 3QA

Hodder & Stoughton

A MEMBER OF THE HODDER HEADLINE GROUP

Acknowledgements

The front cover illustration shows 'Fight Between Carnival and Lent' (1559) by Pieter Bruegel the Elder, Kunsthistorisches Museum, Vienna/AKG London.

The publishers would like to thank the following individuals, institutions and companies for permission to reproduce copyright illustrations in this book: Mary Evans Picture Library pages 31, 45, 56 and 92.

The publishers would also like to thank the following for permission to reproduce material in this book: Blackwell Publishers for the extract from *The Reformation and the English People* by J.J. Scarisbrick, Blackwell Publishers, 1982; Cambridge University Press for the extract from *Poverty & Deviance in Early Modern Europe* by R. Jütte, Cambridge University Press, 1997; Harvard University Press for the extract from *The First Jesuits* by J.W. O'Malley, Harvard University Press, 1993; the Orion Publishing Group for the extract from *The Spanish Inquisition* by Henry Kamen, Weidenfeld and Nicolson, 1998; the extract from *Christianity in the West 1400–1700* by J. Bossy, Oxford University Press, 1985, by permission of Oxford University Press; Ronnie Po-Chia Hsia for the extract from *Social Discipline in the Reformation: Central Europe* by Ronnie Po-Chia Hsia, Routledge, 1989; Routledge for the extract from *The Catholic Reformation* by Michael A. Mullett, Routledge, 1999; T. and T. Clark for the extract from *Collected Works of Thomas Muntzer*, trans. and ed. by P. Matheson, T. and T. Clark, 1998; Taylor & Francis Group plc for the extract from 'The Long Reformation: Catholics, Protestants and the multitude' by E. Duffy in *England's Long Reformation, 1500–1800*, edited by N. Tyacke, UCL, 1998; Yale University Press for the extract from *Luther: Man Between God and the Devil* by H. Oberman, Yale University Press, 1989.

Every effort has been made to trace and acknowledge ownership of copyright. The publishers will be glad to make suitable arrangements with any copyright holders whom it has not been possible to contact.

Orders: please contact Bookpoint Ltd, 130 Milton Park, Abingdon, Oxon OX14 4SB. Telephone (44) 01235 827720, Fax: (44) 01235 400454. Lines are open from 9.00–6.00, Monday to Saturday, with a 24 hour message answering service. Email address: orders@bookpoint.co.uk

British Library Cataloguing in Publication Data
A catalogue record for this title is available from the British Library

ISBN 0 340 781416

First published 2001
Impression number   10 9 8 7 6 5 4 3 2 1
Year   2007 2006 2005 2004 2003 2002 2001

Copyright © 2001 Geoffrey Woodward

All rights reserved. No part of this publication may be reproduced or transmitted in any form or by any means, electronic or mechanical, including photocopy, recording, or any information storage and retrieval system, without permission in writing from the publisher or under licence from the Copyright Licensing Agency Limited. Further details of such licences (for reprographic reproduction) may be obtained from the Copyright Licensing Agency Limited, of 90 Tottenham Court Road, London W1P 9HE.

Typeset by Fakenham Photosetting Limited, Fakenham, Norfolk
Printed in Great Britain for Hodder & Stoughton Educational, a division of Hodder Headline Plc, 338 Euston Road, London NW1 3BH by Bath Press Ltd.

Contents

Preface v

Chapter 1 Introduction 1
    1 The Purpose of the Book 1
    2 The Nature of the Evidence 1
    3 A Question of Definition 2
    4 Historiographical Issues 3
    5 An Overview of the Book 6

Chapter 2 The Condition of the Western Church around 1517 7
    1 The Institutions of the Church 7
    2 Theological Ideas and Heresy 10
    3 Popular Beliefs 13
    4 Criticisms of the Church 17
    5 Evidence of Reform 20
    6 Conclusion 22
    Study Guide 23

Chapter 3 Martin Luther and the German Reformation 25
    1 Germany on the Eve of the Reformation 25
    2 Luther and the Catholic Church 31
    3 Luther's Appeal 37
    Study Guide 43

Chapter 4 Zwinglianism, Radicalism and Calvinism 45
    1 Zwingli and the Swiss Reformation 45
    2 Radical Sects: the Anabaptists 52
    3 Calvin and Geneva 56
    4 Conclusion 62
    Study Guide 63

Chapter 5 The English Reformation 65
    1 Henry VIII and the English Church 65
    2 The Edwardian Reformation, 1547–53 74
    3 The Marian Reformation, 1553–58 78
    4 The Elizabethan Reformation 1558–71 81
    Study Guide 85

Chapter 6 The Catholic Reformation 88
    1 Early Catholic Reform Movements 88
    2 Loyola and the Jesuits 92
    3 The Council of Trent (1545–63) 95
    4 Repression of Heresy 99
    5 Spiritual and Secular Reformers: the Reformation in Italy and Spain 102
    6 Conclusion 105
    Study Guide 107

Chapter 7	The Effects of the Reformation	109
	1 Religious Impact of the Reformation	109
	2 Political Effects of the Reformation	116
	3 Economic Effects	121
	4 Social Effects	124
	5 Culture	129
	Study Guide	132
Further Reading		134
Index		137

Preface

The original *Access to History* series was conceived as a collection of sets of books covering popular chronological periods in British history, together with the histories of other countries, such as France, Germany, Russia and the USA. This arrangement complemented the way in which history has traditionally been taught in sixth forms, colleges and universities. In recent years, however, other ways of dividing up the past have become increasingly popular. In particular, there has been a greater emphasis on studying relatively brief periods in considerable detail and on comparing similar historical phenomena in different countries. These developments have generated a demand for appropriate learning materials, and, in response, two new 'strands' have been added to the main series – *In Depth* and *Themes*. The new volumes build directly on the features that have made *Access to History* so popular.

To the General Reader

Access books have been specifically designed to meet the needs of examination students, but they also have much to offer the general reader. The authors are committed to the belief that good history must not only be accurate, up-to-date and scholarly, but also clearly and attractively written. The main body of the text (excluding the Study Guide sections) should therefore form a readable and engaging survey of a topic. Moreover, each author has aimed not merely to provide as clear an explanation as possible of what happened in the past but also to stimulate readers and to challenge them into thinking for themselves about the past and its significance. Thus, although no prior knowledge is expected from the reader, he or she is treated as an intelligent and thinking person throughout. The author tends to share ideas and explore possibilities, instead of delivering so-called 'historical truths' from on high.

To the student reader

It is intended that *Access* books should be used by students studying history at a higher level. Its volumes are all designed to be working texts, which should be reasonably clear on a first reading but which will benefit from re-reading and close study.

To be an effective and successful student, you need to budget your time wisely. Hence you should think carefully about how important the material in a particular book is for you. If you simply need to acquire a general grasp of a topic, the following approach will probably be effective:

1. Read Chapter 1, which should give you an overview of the whole book, and think about its contents.

2. Skim through Chapter 2, paying particular attention to the 'Points to Consider' box and to the 'Key Issue' highlighted at the start of each section. Decide if you need to read the whole chapter.
3. If you do, read the chapter, stopping at the end of every sub-division of the text to make notes.
4. Repeat stage 2 (and stage 3 where appropriate) for the other chapters.

If, however, your course demands a detailed knowledge of the contents of the book, you will need to be correspondingly more thorough. There is no perfect way of studying, and it is particularly worthwhile experimenting with different styles of note-making to find the one that best suits you. Nevertheless the following plan of action is worth trying:

1. Read a whole chapter quickly, preferably at one sitting. Avoid the temptation – which may be very great – to make notes at this stage.
2. Study the diagram at the end of the chapter, ensuring that you understand the general 'shape' of what you have read.
3. Re-read the chapter more slowly, this time taking notes. You may well be amazed at how much more intelligible and straightforward the material seems on a second reading – and your notes will be correspondingly more useful to you when you have to write an essay or revise for an exam. In the long run, reading a chapter twice can, in fact, often save time. Be sure to make your notes in a clear, orderly fashion, and spread them out so that, if necessary, you can later add extra information.
4. The Study Guide sections will be particularly valuable for those taking AS Level, A Level and Higher. Read the advice on essay questions, and do tackle the specimen titles. (Remember that if learning is to be effective, it must be active. No one – alas – has yet devised any substitute for real effort. It is up to you to make up your own mind on the key issues in any topic.)
5. Attempt the *Source-based questions* section. The guidance on tackling these exercises is well worth reading and thinking about.

When you have finished the main chapters, go through the 'Further Reading' section. Remember that no single book can ever do more than introduce a topic, and it is to be hoped that, time permitting, you will want to read more widely. If *Access* books help you to discover just how diverse and fascinating the human past can be, the series will have succeeded in its aim – and you will experience that enthusiasm for the subject which, along with efficient learning, is the hallmark of the best students.

Robert Pearce

1 Introduction

> **POINTS TO CONSIDER**
>
> This chapter considers the purpose and contents of this book and outlines some of the problems that historians face when researching and writing about the Reformation. How should we define the Reformation and in what ways has recent scholarship changed our understanding of this complex movement?

1 The Purpose of the Book

The aim of this book is fourfold. Firstly, it presents a study of the sixteenth-century European Reformation. Both the continental and English reformations are examined with England, Spain, France, Germany, the Netherlands, Italy and Switzerland providing most of the illustrations. Although the focus is on the western Church, reference is also made to central and eastern Europe, areas that historians now appreciate reveal much about the sixteenth-century reform movements. Secondly, it offers a thematic interpretation of the political, religious, social, economic and cultural effects of the Reformation in the sixteenth century. This enables the reader to judge the pace, depth and variety of reform that existed between states and within individual towns and regions. Thirdly, by drawing upon the most recent studies, it endeavours to provide an up to date analysis of the Reformation. Hundreds of books, articles, theses and papers are published each year on national, regional and local studies. As a result, our perception of the Reformation is quite different from that held by historians a generation ago. Fourthly, it seeks to present a narrative and analytical interpretation of the sixteenth-century Reformation through the use of primary and secondary sources, and offers advice and exercises for students on how to answer documentary and essay questions.

2 The Nature of the Evidence

A major problem facing the historian of the Reformation is the fragmentary nature of the surviving evidence. Visitation records, for instance, which contain material concerning parish and diocesan affairs, often have more gaps than entries. Where evidence has survived, it is often biased towards church and lay officials and is not necessarily typical of what ordinary people thought. Evidence of heresy trials, diocesan visitations and ecclesiastical courts, for example, all contain details of individuals who were untypical or unorthodox. The case of a London merchant, Richard Hunne, who was accused of heresy, arrested by the Church and found murdered in his cell in 1514, attracted wide attention at the time but was an exceptional example of clerical corruption and heresy. The clergy did not usually treat suspected heretics so outrageously and few heretics were as rich or as prickly as Hunne. Of course, the majority of people conformed and details of their lives went unrecorded. We therefore only know about those who came before the authorities or, in a minority of cases, had their feelings documented in a letter or will. Since most people were illiterate and left no record of their opinions, forming judgements on limited evidence is difficult and full of pitfalls.

In the past, historians have placed much emphasis on the study of wills because they contain details of a testator's possessions and state of mind as he or she neared their death, but even wills are problematical. Were they written by the testator or a scribe? English wills, for example, were drawn up by clerics, French wills by notaries, and a study of wills from Cordoba (Castile) reveals that little was ever left to charitable purposes since it was customary to give donations throughout one's life rather than in a bequest. Since wills were mainly penned by old, dying and wealthy people, they were hardly typical of society and their views may well have changed in the course of their life. Are indications of Christian piety, Catholic orthodoxy or Lutheran beliefs, genuine sentiments or responses to social and legal conventions? We simply cannot tell.

If we take examples of anti-clericalism, the evidence may suggest that there was widespread clerical abuse, but an alternative interpretation is that the Church was quite sound except, of course, in the eyes of the complainants who saw it falling short of their expectations. Is evidence of criticism, therefore, a sign of strength or corruption? When Erasmus condemned various clerical practices, many people may have agreed with him but few embarked on a campaign of church reform; and when English Puritans urged Elizabeth to reform the prayer book, they gained little support from the rest of the country that was quite content with church doctrine as it stood. Conversely, the absence of complaint does not mean that people were totally satisfied with their church and clergy. Fear of retribution, both socially and legally, will have impelled cooperation and silence in many cases. Moreover, when people did express their opinions by word or deed, it is likely they had mixed motives. For example, religious inspired demonstrations, revolts and rebellions, were never just about religion; social and economic grievances were often as important, or even more important, factors in causing popular revolts.

3 A Question of Definition

The term 'Reformation' is a much used concept and, like other historical labels such as 'Renaissance' and 'Enlightenment', has been much abused. In the Middle Ages, a *'reformatio'* occurred when a university faculty was restored to its original condition, and this is what Luther would have understood by its usage. When he introduced changes to the Catholic Church, Luther never saw himself as a reformer, nor did he ever claim to have begun a 'Reformation'. In the seventeenth century, the term was used to describe a historical period between 1517, when Luther criticised the sale of indulgences, and 1555, when religious conflict in Germany was ended by the peace of Augsburg. The centrality of Luther was stressed by eighteenth-century German historians, a view endorsed by the growth and appeal of liberalism and nationalism in the following century.

The term 'Counter-Reformation' also became current in the nineteenth century. It implied that a Catholic reaction occurred directly as a result of the German Reformation. This idea that the Reformation was primarily a religious and political movement, that it was responsible for improving the Christian Church, and that it had clear parameters, only came to be questioned and re-defined in the twentieth century. Historians have shown, for example, that the Catholic Church owed its revival in the sixteenth century largely to its own initiatives, some of which preceded Luther, and that the phrase 'Catholic Reformation' or 'Catholic Renewal' may be a more accurate description than 'Counter-Reformation'.

The term 'Protestant Reformation' has also presented a problem. Coined in 1529 when a small number of German princes and imperial cities protested at not being allowed to practise Lutheran beliefs, by 1530 a 'protestant' was one who agreed to the Augsburg Confession, and thereafter anyone who rejected the Catholic faith. In reality, many Christians who shared Luther's view that the Bible should be the basis of their faith, rejected some of his other beliefs, as well as those of rival faiths, but were still called Protestant as a term of abuse by their Catholic opponents. Indeed, 'Zwinglian', 'Calvinist', 'Anabaptist' and 'puritan' were also derogatory terms.

4 Historiographical Issues

Until the twentieth century, most historians viewed the Reformation as a religious-political event which was mainly inspired by the intellectual and spiritual drive of individual preachers. Luther, Zwingli, Calvin, Cranmer and Loyola, held centre stage and historical interpretations were often coloured by nationalist, confessional and moral considerations. The role of the individual in shaping events still holds a fascination for historians and biographies of the leading reformers have spawned more than their fair share of controversial interpretations. Let us take Luther as an example, and, in particular, consider what transformed this obscure university lecturer into public enemy number one (as far as the papacy was concerned). Erik Erikson saw Luther's relationship with his father as the key to understanding his real and psychological crisis; Norman Brown explained his spiritual anxieties as a result of pathological constipation; Heiko Oberman believed Luther had a fixation with God; and Richard Marius, his most recent biographer, considered his life was governed by his fear of death.

Historians have long acknowledged Luther's contributions to the Reformation but recent studies have been more cautious in their praise. No longer is it accepted that Luther 'began' the Reformation or that all other reformations sprang from him. The significance of other contemporary German preachers such as Karlstadt, Müntzer, Bucer, Osiander, Melanchthon and Bugenhagen, was often as great if not greater than Luther's, and in southern Germany and Switzerland Zwingli was the more popular reformer. Moreover, he developed his ideas independently of Luther. It is no longer accepted that people were inevitably won over to Lutheranism or that the movement was unquestionably successful. Luther himself held grave reservations about how to proceed and was deeply upset by the limited impact of his reforms. Although historians remain uncertain about the success of Lutheranism, studies of Strasbourg and Nuremberg suggest that his challenge to traditional Catholic beliefs was better received than Luther realised. It is no longer accepted that the 'Luther affair' began the modern age and provided the seedbed of capitalism and rationalism. In questioning the Church's views on money lending, for instance, he inevitably encouraged others to think how far this practice could be morally justified, but this issue was only a minor part in the development of capitalist theory. Similarly, by obliging people to re-consider their spiritual beliefs, he provoked many to go in search of the truth but this quest for knowledge was only part of a much longer process begun by the Renaissance. Finally, it is no longer accepted that Luther was a saint, a prophet or a liberator; these were images that his followers did so much to propagate and which nineteenth-century German historians readily repeated.

Marxist historians have always stressed the importance of social and economic factors in our understanding of the past and, if their political explanations of the sixteenth century have not always stood up to scrutiny, there is no doubt that modern research has benefited from the study of urban history, social groups and popular culture. Whether, as some historians have claimed, the German Reformation was a 'people's reformation', a 'communal reformation', an 'urban event' or a 'princely reformation', it is clear that different political and cultural conditions in Germany produced a variety of reformations. A similar picture was evident outside Germany. The historiography of the English Reformation in the last half century is a good example of just how much our understanding of the Reformation has changed. Historians writing in the 1960s, for instance, argued that the Church had lost its way and most people were tired of clerical corruption and mechanistic rituals, such as donating money to the Church, saying payers for the dead or going on pilgrimages. Twenty years later this view was challenged by scholars who claimed that, far from being a popular anti-clerical movement, the Reformation was initiated by the state for essentially political and economic reasons. In the words of Jack Scarisbrick: 'The English people neither wanted nor welcomed the Reformation.' Present-day writers still regard the continental reforms as mainly peripheral to what happened in England, and suspect that pressure for reform came from a section of the laity that wished to exercise more control over the Church. Our understanding of the appeal of Calvinism has also been revised in recent years due to the investigation of local and town archives in France and the Netherlands. Whether or not Calvinism took root and survived often owed more to prevailing social and political conditions than to any inherent qualities implicit in the church's organisation. Studies of eastern and central Europe have shown that areas outside the heartland of the Reformation were often very receptive to reformist ideas. Lutherans, Anabaptists, Calvinists and Jesuits all found success in spreading their ideas and historians are only just beginning to appreciate why states like Bohemia, Moravia, Hungary and Poland responded to the Protestant and Catholic impulses from the West.

Historians now have a much better picture of the origin, development and rate of progress made by reform movements in the sixteenth century. Although there remains plenty of scope for disagreement, a consensus has been achieved on a number of issues. Firstly, there was nothing inevitable about the Reformation. The view that the Roman Catholic Church was a corrupt institution waiting to be reformed was Protestant propaganda. Recent historians, who have concentrated their research on the late fifteenth-century Church, have concluded that it was in a reasonably healthy condition. It may not have been perfect (few multi-national institutions are) but it was not facing a crisis. Secondly, the Catholic Reformation preceded Luther but only really took off in the seventeenth century. The traditional view held by many Catholic historians that the Catholic Reformation began with the Council of Trent (1545–63) is no longer tenable. The Reformation was a long, slow process for Protestants and Catholics alike. Thirdly, there was great diversity and variation in reforms from town to town and from country to country. In Sweden, England, Spain and France, for example, the initiative for change lay in the hands of the monarchy; in Germany, Switzerland, Italy and the Netherlands, political and social conditions mainly accounted for the variety of practices. The extent to which change was continuous or intermittent, fast or slow, depended upon individual rulers, parish preachers and communal groups. Fourthly, less emphasis is now placed on the role of Luther and more on contemporary reformers. This is not to diminish Luther's contribution to the Reformation but to set him in a broader perspective. Modern studies on the Anabaptists, for instance, show that they should be regarded as part of the mainstream reformation and not marginalised as fringe groups because they did not fit in with Luther's conservative views.

5 An Overview of the Book

Chapter 2 provides an assessment of the condition of the western Church around 1517 when Luther first challenged orthodox teaching. It considers the existing beliefs, customs and institutions of the Catholic Church, and the attempts by humanists, scholars and preachers to jolt the papacy out of its lethargy. How and why Luther was able to generate so much support in Germany between 1517 and 1521, and the way he subsequently had to adapt to changing circumstances, is the focus of Chapter 3. He was undoubtedly the spark which initiated so many changes in the sixteenth century and is the most important figure you will encounter in this book. The theological ideas and popular appeal of the other main continental Protestant movements – Zwinglianism, Anabaptism and Calvinism – are the subject of Chapter 4. Historians now acknowledge that the decade following the death of Luther in 1546 was a critical time for European Protestants: Zwinglianism had lost its impetus, Lutheranism was becoming stale, Anabaptism was deemed to be too subversive, and Calvinism was in its infancy. In addition, there were many varieties of reform movements competing for Protestant converts, or simply trying to survive. Chapter 5 examines the English Reformation. It considers its origins and main developments, as well as its links with the continental reformation. It is treated here in a separate chapter because it was a unique event caused not by dissatisfaction with the Church's theological teaching but by the papacy refusing to grant Henry VIII a divorce. How far and why the Catholic Church recovered from its ailing condition in the face of the Protestant assault, and the nature of its revival, is the focus of Chapter 6. To some, the Catholic reformer, Loyola, who founded the Jesuits, was more important than either Luther or Calvin. The final chapter takes a thematic look at the consequences of the Protestant and Catholic reformations and examines their impact on religious, political, economic, social and cultural affairs.

2 The Condition of the Christian Church in Western Europe around 1517

POINTS TO CONSIDER

The Roman Catholic Church exercised considerable power in western Europe in the later Middle Ages. This chapter examines its institutions, theology and personnel, and its relationship with secular authorities. It looks at popular beliefs that were legitimised by the Church and those that were not. Finally, it considers the nature of anti-clericalism and sets the complaints concerning the clergy and papacy against a background of popular piety, Christian humanism and reform movements. As you make your way through the sections of this chapter, try to decide why the Church was considered by some to be in need of reform and by others to be perfectly satisfactory. What is your opinion?

KEY DATES

1054	Catholic Church divided into western and eastern churches.
1343	Treasury of Merits acknowledged by the papacy.
1348–49	Black Death.
1378–1417	Great Schism.
1471	Pontificate of Sixtus IV (until 1484).
1492	Pontificate of Alexander VI (until 1503).
1503	Pontificate of Julius II (until 1513).
1512	Fifth Lateran Council met in Rome.
1513	Pontificate of Leo X (until 1521).

1 The Institutions of the Church

KEY ISSUE What were the principal institutions of the Roman Catholic Church?

a) The Papacy

The Christian Church was described in the fourth century Nicene Creed as 'one, holy, catholic and apostolic': it was a Church, united in faith and headship, that believed in the preaching and spreading of Catholic ideas. Since then it had seen many changes. In 1054 internal disagreements caused it to split into a western Latin Church headed by the pope in Rome, and an eastern Greek organisation led by the patriarch in Constantinople. The thirteenth century brought substantial reforms that included the emergence of friars and the spread of Christianity throughout western and central Europe. Heretical ideas which challenged its teaching and authority presented serious problems in the Middle Ages, and the early fifteenth century, which witnessed the Great Schism (1378–1417), when two and for a short period three men claimed to be pope, was one of the lowest points in its history. Nevertheless, the Church survived due to the strength of its institutions and its capacity to adapt to changing circumstances. In 1517 the Roman Catholic Church seemed omnipotent.

The pope, as bishop of Rome, claimed to be the representative on earth of St Peter, one of the disciples who had allegedly died in Rome. Although the pope did not claim infallibility, he did not expect to be challenged on spiritual matters. He was elected and advised by a college of cardinals but, once in office, he exercised total power. Some popes, like Sixtus IV, abused the office and appointed friends and relatives as cardinals. Similarly the papal curia, the court housing domestic and administrative offices, and the Chancery, where papal letters and decrees were issued, were filled with clients and relatives of the cardinals. Indeed the curia had trebled in size in the early sixteenth century to over 700 servants and there was a lively trade in purchasing posts. Leo X alone was responsible for selling some 2,000 offices.

The pope's authority rested on the Bible, Roman Law and customary practice. Customary law was based on local and seigneurial traditions, and treated the accused with greater consideration than Roman Law, which was founded on authoritarian principles and favoured the prosecutor. However, not everyone accepted the basis of papal power. General councils of the Church, for example, claimed to be Christ's representative on earth and responsible for administering the Church. Moreover, one such council that had met in 1415 declared that it was superior to the pope, and subsequent councils met independently of him to undertake reforms. The papacy recovered from this chastening experience – the last council met in 1449 – and subsequently denounced general councils as inferior, but the prospect remained that another one could be easily convened. The papacy's reputation had also been damaged by two other episodes. First, in the 1440s the Donation of Constantine (an alleged fourth-century imperial decree), which gave so much power to the papacy, was found to be an eighth-century forgery; second, in the 1490s Alexander VI became involved in international politics by encouraging a French army to invade Italy. The pope hoped to expand his own lands, the Papal States, and his conduct and that of his successor, Julius II who took to the field with his army, seemed to many to be a dereliction of spiritual headship.

The threat of a general council and the political ambitions of the Renaissance popes put the papacy on the defensive and largely accounts for the growth of state churches in the course of the fifteenth century. European states such as France, England, Spain, Portugal and Scotland, seized their chance to gain and extend control over religious affairs – to appoint clerics, pocket taxes and impose their will over their clergy. The Concordat of Bologna of 1516, for example, allowed the French crown the right to nominate all priors, abbots and bishops, while the pope would confirm them and receive taxation. In practice, the king controlled episcopal and monastic patronage, as well as ecclesiastical property, and allowed the pope only as much tax as he felt was appropriate. Papal relations with Germany, however, were different. Although agreements had been made with several German princes in 1448, they exerted less influence over clerical appointments and, in the absence of a unitary state or an emperor who could command universal respect, papal power in Germany remained strong.

b) The Clergy

The harmony of church-state relations and the effectiveness of church administration rested largely upon the clerical hierarchy – the archbishops, bishops, deans and abbots. The primate – the archbishops of Canterbury in England, Rheims in France and Toledo in Castile, for instance – was appointed by the crown and approved by the papacy. Assisting him were a number of fellow bishops: France had 15 archbishops and 88 bishops, England 2 and 15, and Italy as many as 27 archbishops and more than 200 bishops. According to canon law, archbishops were required to call provincial assemblies every three years and bishops were to undertake frequent visitations. In practice, this rarely happened because most bishops were also expected to assist their king in diplomatic and administrative duties and so were frequently absent from their dioceses (areas of administration).The size of their dioceses varied considerably. In Italy they were mainly small and carried low salaries but in France and Germany they were generally large and wealthy and attracted the sons of the gentry and nobility.

Bishops were responsible for the spiritual and pastoral conduct of the secular and regular clergy. Since many parish clergy received low salaries – averaging £8 a year in England, compared with a bishop's income of some £2,000 – they often held additional offices and it is not hard to see why many clerics were accused of pluralism. Most parishes in Europe had a superfluity of unbeneficed clergymen. In England and Wales, in addition to the 9,000 parish priests, there were some 40,000 chantry priests who sang masses for the souls of the departed. France also appears to have had many poorly paid *curés* who assisted in the large parishes. It had four times as many parishes as England and the number of men entering the priesthood continued to rise, perhaps due to the legal and tax privileges accorded to men in holy orders. For instance, over a thousand were ordained in 1514 in the Séez diocese of Normandy. The priest's workload was excessive. In addition to conducting daily services and preaching a weekly sermon, he was expected to be a pastor, teacher, and provider of spiritual relief, ministering the sacraments to one and all, from the cradle to the grave.

Fewer men and women were entering monastic life in the early sixteenth century; its heyday had been the twelfth and thirteenth centuries when most foundations were made. Many smaller institutions had high debts, only a few inmates, and were struggling to survive. In contrast, some of the larger monasteries appeared to have too much income and operated like real estate managers. The larger monasteries and convents not surprisingly were run as businesses. Glastonbury, for example, had property all over England and an annual income in excess of £4,000. Moreover, most monks and friars had relaxed the rules governing their orders (known as 'conventuals'), although this trend was reversed in the fifteenth century by 'observants', who sought to return to their original status. The Observant Benedictine houses in Melk (Austria), St Matthias (Trier) and Monte Cassino (Italy), were renowned for their strictness, as were many of the 700 Cistercian and 200 Carthusian houses. Similarly, the Observant Dominican, Franciscan and Augustinian orders continued to attract many patrons and novices. Nuns belonged to either the Carmelite order dedicated to poverty, abstinence and solitude or to one of the sister houses run by a monastery. A new order of Bridgettines based on meditative prayer, piety and self-denial, had also started in the fifteenth century. Some, like Syon Abbey in London, acquired an international reputation for monastic idealism. The contribution monasteries made to a community must have been variable. At best, they fulfilled an important educational, charitable and spiritual role complementing the work of lay institutions and the parish priest; at worst, they were avaricious landlords, living off the fat of the land, who gave little to the community at large.

2 Theological Ideas and Heresy

> **KEY ISSUES** What were the main orthodox beliefs of the Catholic faith? Why were some people heretics?

a) The Seven Sacraments and Purgatory

The official faith of the Christian Church rested on the three creeds of the Apostles, Nicene and St Athanasius, formulated in 325, and on moral precepts drawn from the Ten Commandments and the New Testament. It is important to recognise that while orthodox beliefs were grounded upon these works many theological ideas remained undefined and open to interpretation. Although western Christendom presented itself as a church with common values, it contained in fact a variety of theological beliefs and practices which at times seemed paradoxical. It could, on the one hand, tolerate popular deviations from the orthodox faith, and then, if it perceived they posed a threat to the unity and leadership of the Church, condemn them as heretical.

The seven sacraments lay at the heart of the Christian faith. Baptism protected the new born child from evil spirits and conferred grace on the baptised. The second sacrament, confirmation, anointed the baptised with holy oil and secured their full admission to the Church. Marriage was the third sacrament. Although it did not require priestly participation, if it was conducted or witnessed by a priest, then grace was conferred on the couple. Extreme unction, the fourth sacrament, was the blessing given in the final moments of a person's life. The fifth, penance, was an act of atonement for sinful behaviour and a compulsory rite performed at least once a year. The Eucharist, the sixth sacrament, was holy communion in which the wine and bread were blessed by a priest, thereby consecrating the elements into the blood and body of Christ, an act known as transubstantiation. The laity was given bread only, whereas the clergy took communion 'in both kinds'. Finally, ordination was a sacrament available to those men who wished to enter minor or holy orders.

Although all seven sacraments were theoretically of equal merit, in the course of the fifteenth century baptism, penance and the Eucharist came to be regarded as the most important. This reflected popular attitudes towards sin and death, heaven and hell, attitudes which were reinforced by the Church's teaching. The act of baptism established the infant as part of the Church and society but, once this sacrament had taken place, penance and the Eucharist assumed greater significance in adult lives. Sins could only be partially forgiven and the procedure, which was in four stages, was far from easy. First, the penitent had to be contrite, second confess to a priest, and third fulfil a punishment to the satisfaction of the priest, before finally receiving absolution. Since you were not permitted to take communion until you had first confessed, this sacrament assumed vital significance. Manuals instructing people how to prepare for confession became essential reading both for the laity and clergy, since the latter had to be sure that the penitent was spiritually ready to confess and then impose the appropriate disciplinary punishments. These could range from reciting a number of Hail Maries to undertaking a pilgrimage, or working with the sick and poor.

Central to belief in this penitential system was the concept of purgatory. This was a place where the dead waited for their souls to be purged of sin before going to heaven or hell. Christ had died for mankind; now mankind must seek salvation on earth before paying for one's sins in purgatory. The Church Triumphant were already in heaven; the Church Dormant were in purgatory; and the Church Militant were earth-bound and in need of constant repentance. Moreover, there was no guarantee that those souls in purgatory would ever enter heaven. The Church was also unclear in explaining precisely what could be done to help the sinner. A fifth-century theologian, St Augustine, believed that man was destined to suffer since God alone could grant salvation. Acts of charity and worthy deeds, he argued, had no bearing on his fate. This view was endorsed by most churchmen and scholars in the Middle Ages although some, like William of Occam, suggested that God was more likely to save a man from sin if his life on earth showed merit. Charitable acts and good deeds were not therefore irrelevant. This academic issue was of marginal importance to most people but exercised the minds of reformation theologians for years to come. At the beginning of the sixteenth century, however, the Church stressed the importance of regular confession, celebrating mass and performing charitable deeds.

Since purgatory was unavoidable and you did not know how long your soul would spend there, the burning question was: how could you lessen this torment? The Church's answer lay in the Treasury of Merits, formally acknowledged by the papacy in 1343. It was claimed that Christ's sacrifice on the cross was so great that it had built up unlimited merits which were now at the Church's disposal. You would therefore be rewarded if you requested masses for the dead, visited the shrines of saints, performed acts of charity or bought indulgences. Initially made available to those who went on crusades, indulgences were letters that secured a partial remission of sin for the purchaser as well as for anyone else they named. In 1476 their popularity grew enormously when the papacy announced that the souls of the departed could also be included in these letters. Not only would the dead be assisted, the living would be rewarded through this act of consideration.

b) Heresy

Not everyone accepted the Church's theology. In south-east France and north-west Italy, the Waldenses had questioned the doctrine of purgatory and papal authority. Pursued by the state and church authorities, by 1517 they were confined to Dauphiné and Provence, and were no longer considered a problem. Indeed, only four Waldenses were accused of heresy in the Toulouse *parlement* between 1511 and 1520. The Hussites in Bohemia proved more difficult to suppress. John Hus had been burned at the stake in 1415 but his followers survived in force. They adopted the Scriptures and Christian precepts as their sole authority, used a vernacular Bible, and advocated communion in both kinds for the laity. Although they were consistently condemned by the papacy, the Holy Roman Emperor had granted them the right to practise their beliefs in prescribed areas of

Bohemia. The third heretical group – the Lollards – were also confined to one country. These English followers of John Wyclif, a fourteenth-century Oxford scholar, rejected transubstantiation, indulgences, pilgrimages, clerical celibacy, the sacred condition of the priesthood and the papacy. At the heart of their beliefs lay the English Bible, which had been translated from the Latin Vulgate. They presented a most serious challenge to orthodox views and both the state and church took steps to repress them. By the early sixteenth century, they were largely confined to communities in London, Kent, Coventry and the Chilterns, and were forced to worship in secret. Occasionally, suspects were rounded up and tried for heresy. For example, 74 people appeared before the bishop of Coventry between 1510 and 1512 and, in London, Coventry and Kent, a handful of burnings took place to purge them of their heretical sins.

Heresy was not a problem for the Church at the beginning of the sixteenth century. Heretical groups had been contained and their leaders condemned. This clearly demonstrates how effectively opposition could be suppressed when the Church and secular authorities worked together: in France and England, for example, suspects were arrested, tried and sentenced by the Church, and then executed by the state. Elsewhere, in Germany, Italy, Spain and Portugal, inquisitions had been established and, although most fell into abeyance in the fifteenth century, Castile and Aragon set up permanent tribunals in the 1480s.

3 Popular Beliefs

> **KEY ISSUES** What were the main beliefs and customs of the common people? What theological ideas lay behind them?

a) Death and the Millennium

There is no better illustration of the wide diversity of religious practices in western Europe than a study of popular beliefs. Some bordered on superstition, pagan and magical ideas but most practices were legitimised by the Church. Death and the prospect of dying held centre stage. If stories of the Black Death did not demonstrate the uncertainty of life, there were sufficient reminders from preachers and actors, in church and in literature, of the certainty of death. The *Art of Dying Well*, for instance, was a German handbook of 1416 which went through 23 editions by 1500; and the *Dance Macabre*, which showed the slaughter of the Maccabees, was a favourite play. Sculptured gargoyles with distorted faces, paintings depicting souls in torment, stained glass windows, rood screens (wooden or stone carved screens which separated the nave from the chancel) and altarpieces showing saints in heaven, all conveyed vivid images to the

Church Militant. At Fairford, Gloucestershire, for example, a stained glass painting showed souls in a wheelbarrow being carried to hell; and at St Andrew's church, Cullompton, Devon, a carved statue of Christ on the Cross, with death-heads at the foot of the rood, looked down upon the congregation. The approach of the half-millennium in 1500 added to people's anxiety. Some believed that the world would end when the Jews were converted to Christianity, which made their persecution in Iberia in the 1490s particularly ominous. Others forecast a new world order and an anonymous German text, the *Reformatio Sigismundi*, predicted an 'Imperatur' would reform the Church. That the Antichrist did not appear in 1500 did not discourage soothsayers from declaring that the Second Coming was only a matter of time!

b) Holy Days

The celebration of holy days and feast days afforded a good opportunity for people to participate in the solemnised rituals of the church calendar. Most countries celebrated nearly 100 festival days; Germany had 161. Civic processions were attended by the laity and clergy, rich and poor, to affirm their communal unity. In Venice, it was held on St Mark's day; in England on St George's day and in Florence on St John the Baptist's day. Holy days often combined pagan and Christian rituals. The end of winter, for instance, and the purification of the Blessed Virgin Mary was marked by Candlemas on 2 February. Corpus Christi fell on a Thursday in June and was accompanied by fairs, passion plays and processions. In Spain, the Mystery of Elche about Mary's Assumption was a popular drama, and at York a series of plays told the biblical story and imparted lessons of morality. All Souls' day on 2 November commemorated the souls of the dead by warding off evil spirits that had been abroad at Hallowe'en.

c) Saints, Relics and Pilgrimages

The cult of saints was a widespread activity. Some were patron saints authorised by the Church, like St James in Spain and St George in England. Others had biblical origins, like St Anne and the Virgin Mary, but the majority were local saints venerated by villages and towns throughout Europe. The patron saint of Mijas near Malaga in Spain, the Ermita Virgen de la Peña, which dated back to the ninth century, was not untypical. People became attached to particular saints as a form of protection: St Sebastian kept the plague away; St Christopher protected travellers; and St Apollonia fended off toothache. Although the Church was keen that relics of saints should not be worshipped or used in magical rites, they were avidly collected, carried and revered since the closer you got to the remnants of a saint, the more they saved you from sin. Chartres held the Virgin

Mary's veil, Lyon cathedral the jaw of St John, and St Denis in Paris had the Crown of Thorns. In Germany, Trier cathedral had the robe of Christ, Augsburg claimed to have a 'Bleeding host' and Wittenberg Castle church in Saxony collected an impressive 17,443 holy relics. Many claims were patently false: several churches swore that they possessed fragments of the True Cross, milk of the Virgin Mary, phials of Christ's Blood and the head of John the Baptist, but the Church was unconcerned.

Pilgrimages were extremely popular. Every country had a principal shrine which became the venue for annual holidays. The main international sites were at Jerusalem and Bethlehem but Compostela in Castile, Walsingham in England, Aachen and Wilsnack in Germany, Lourdes and Chartres in France, and St Peter's in Rome were also favoured centres. Motives for going on a pilgrimage varied. Some pilgrims, like Henry VIII who travelled to Walsingham, went on a personal quest; others did so as a form of penance or judicial punishment. 1500 was a special year and saw several 'jubilee' pilgrimages, including one for children, who travelled from all over France to Mont-St.Michel in Brittany.

d) Indulgences, Chantries and Confraternities

Indulgences were bought and sold all over Europe and were particularly in demand in England and Germany. St Anthony's hospital in London sold 30,000 a year and the Guild of St Mary in Boston, Lincolnshire, paid £3,200 for their documents. The cost varied according to the demand and reason for its promulgation. The Jubilee indulgence of 1500, for example, was a special occasion and the pope hoped to use the money to fund a crusade against the Turks as well as to help restore St Peter's cathedral. Each indulgence cost between 4d (1.67p) and £3 6s 8d (£3.33p) according to the status of the buyer. And the more you paid, the greater the remission in purgatory. A reduction of 80,000 days was assured any Spaniard who fasted on the feast days of the Virgin of Cubas, and cardinal Albert of Brandenburg believed that he had bought 39 million years off purgatory with his indulgences.

Chantries and confraternities were even more popular than indulgences because they were readily available to every member of the community. The fourteenth and fifteenth centuries had seen hundreds of thousands of chantries established throughout Europe. Founded in cathedrals, churches, chapels and colleges, chantries were prayers for the dead sung by priests on a daily, monthly and annual basis, according to the terms of the endowment. People gave their priest whatever they could afford. Cash, goods and cattle were given in rural areas, and at Yeovil a white swan was one of several endowments. More permanent chantries were founded with land but this practice was less common at the beginning of the sixteenth century, due partly to the cost and partly to the legal procedures which accompanied land bequests. Nevertheless, wealthy benefactors continued to establish permanent endowments in their wills: in 1509 Henry VII made elaborate provisions at Westminster and other abbeys for 10,000 masses to be said for his departed soul.

Nearly every parish in England and Wales, and most parishes on the continent, possessed a guild or confraternity, which fulfilled both religious and secular functions. In return for an annual subscription, members were assured that prayers would be said for them even if they could not afford an individual endowment. In London, 34 companies headed by the Merchant Taylors sponsored priests in over 60 parish churches. Even in small market towns like Shrewsbury, their three churches were patronised by seven local guilds. Some guilds had a national following and a few, like those in Florence and Venice, had international support. Confraternities had originated in Italy in the fifteenth century. These were principally devotional organisations, and often dedicated to St Anne, but members also undertook to look after each other socially and charitably, and the practice soon spread throughout Europe. Thus at Strasbourg and Braunau, prayer groups belonged to the confraternity of St Ursula, and at Lincoln the Corpus Christi guild was dedicated to the Virgin Mary. Whether lay or religious, these guilds and confraternities brought people together to remember the dead, celebrate mass, and, on Corpus Christi day, carry the host around the town in a procession.

e) Magic and Miracles

Most people whether educated or illiterate believed in the Devil, ghosts, witches and spirits, both good and evil. The Church did not condemn these beliefs but instead provided appropriate sacramentals, such as holy water, palms, candles, oil and salt, to safeguard people from evil. Popular usage, of course, ensured that prayers readily became incantations, and incantations could conjure up magic. It was believed therefore that images of saints when immersed in rivers would bring rain; that horses bled by a farrier would cure illness; that the ringing of bells was a protection against lightning. Thus at Aardenburg in Flanders, fishermen put their statue of Our Lady into the sea when there were storms, and at Friuli in Italy the *benandanti* (witch-beaters) on quarter days waged nightly battles to defend their children. In 1484 the papacy had declared witchcraft a heresy and tried to stamp out related practices but to many the line between incantations and prayers, and between supernatural magic and Christian miracles, seemed less certain and could not be so readily dismissed. It is not surprising to find, therefore, that the *Book of Hours* – a compendium of prayers and recitations – remained compulsive reading, or that miracles continued to be reported and stories about them published. Ringing bells, blessing fields, saying magical charms, and chasing witches may not seem particularly spiritual to us, but it worked for most early sixteenth-century people, lay and clerical, educated and uneducated, and that is what mattered to them.

4 Criticisms of the Church

> **KEY ISSUE** Why did people criticise the Church and how far were these complaints justified?

a) Anti-papalism and Anti-clericalism

The principal criticisms levelled at the papacy were that the Renaissance popes, especially Alexander VI, Julius II and Leo X, were devoid of moral principles, that they showed little interest in church reform and devoted too much time and money to secular pursuits. In addition, the curia was corrupt, papal taxes were resented and appeals to Rome were slow and expensive. While all of these complaints held true, the depth of anti-papal feeling varied considerably. In Germany, for example, it was strong. Many benefices and monastic offices were in the gift of the pope, over one-third of all property belonged to the Church, and towns resented having to pay high legal charges and taxes. Moreover there was no central authority to resist papal demands. Elsewhere, however, there was very little resentment or grievance. In fact, most countries enjoyed a good relationship with the papacy. The early Tudors, for instance, received licences and dispensations upon request, and paid a miserly £4,000 a year in papal taxes; similarly, in France and Spain, the crown held on to a good proportion of papal taxation.

Anti-clericalism, on the other hand, was more persistent and widespread. Simony, the selling of offices, and nepotism, the favouring of relatives, were common abuses in the Church. Sixtus IV, for example, created his nephew archbishop of Avignon and Alexander VI built up lands in central Italy for his son, Caesar Borgia. Appointing under-age children to clerical offices was a blatant abuse, and it went on at the highest levels. The archbishop of Saragossa was nine years old when his father, Ferdinand of Aragon, secured him this position and Jean of Lorraine was only three when he became bishop of Metz. Absenteeism was also a serious problem among the ranks of the upper clergy. Many cathedral canons, bishops and abbots studied at university or served as diplomats and were inevitably away from their offices for long periods of time. Each of the seven bishops of Cordoba between 1476 and 1510, for instance, was a royal administrator and frequently absent on business. In England, Richard Fox never visited his dioceses of Exeter and Bath and Wells between 1487 and 1494, nor did Wolsey visit York following his appointment in 1514, although, in their defence, they did appoint competent deputies to fulfil the sacramental duties. Pluralism was also a source of criticism. Many pluralists felt justified because their clerical income was so low, and the practice was certainly widespread. In England, more than 20 per cent of Lincoln parishes were held by pluralists between 1514 and 1520 but significantly only seven out of 1085 churches had no cleric. In Germany fewer than 10 per cent of priests resided in their parishes but vacancies appear to have been filled by chaplains and curates. However, in much of rural France and Italy, pluralism resulted in minimal pastoral care and there were frequent complaints that there was no priest to meet the spiritual needs of the people.

The moral behaviour of the clergy was another source of criticism. Most bishops were well educated and took their responsibilities seriously but a few were patently corrupt. James Stanley, the bishop of Ely, for example, fathered three illegitimate children; Paul Ziegler, bishop of Chur in Switzerland, selected his mistresses from nunneries in his diocese; and Benedictine nuns in Galicia, Spain, were said to have notoriously loose morals. Of course, the remote and arcane world of monasticism must have encouraged tongues to gossip; and inevitably some monks and nuns did not uphold their traditional vows of honesty, chastity and obedience. Nevertheless, apart from occasional complaints recorded in some German and English towns, cases of sexual misconduct appear to have been rare.

Church courts and privileges enjoyed by clerics could also cause resentment. The right to be tried by canon law – known as benefit of clergy – often secured for the cleric a lenient sentence and was condemned by lawyers who practised in the common law courts where punishments were much harsher. Legal wrangles sometimes occurred if the clergy tried to raise tithe (10 per cent tax) payments or commute farm produce into cash and clerical exemption from civic laws and taxes was a source of anti-clericalism in many German towns. High fees charged for reading wills and conducting burials also gave rise to occasional complaints and was the cause of a bitter dispute between Richard Hunne and the bishop of London between 1511 and 1515. Overall, however, there is little evidence of any sustained anti-clerical campaign by lawyers or laymen on the eve of the Reformation.

b) The Complainants

Throughout the Middle Ages the Church was criticised by laymen and by preachers but the volume appeared to be rising in the fifteenth century. German dramas such as *The Rise and Fall of Antichrist*, in which the Church showed itself incapable of resisting the Devil's temptation, and Sebastian Brant's *Ship of Fools*, which satirised monastic orders, proved highly popular. In England, Chaucer's *Canterbury Tales* and Langland's *Piers Plowman*, portrayed recognisable figures from clerical life. Monastic abuses, ignorant priests and a Church riddled with worldly corruption, were some of the themes that flowed from Erasmus's pen in the early sixteenth century. 'Monasticism is not holiness but a kind of life that can be useful or useless depending on a person's temperament or disposition', he declared. Cardinals were condemned in *In Praise of Folly*: 'For them ... teaching the people is too like hard work, interpreting the holy Scriptures is for academics, and praying is a waste of time.' Papal corruption was the central theme of *Julius Exclusus*, in which the pope was refused entry to the gates of heaven on account of his pleasure-seeking life. And indulgences were the target of Erasmus's attack in the *Enchiridion*. He warned: 'You believe by chance all your sins and offences will be washed away at once with a little paper or parchment sealed with wax, with a little money or images of wax offered, with going on a little pilgrimage. You are utterly deceived'.

In England, John Colet and Thomas More voiced their criticisms in contrasting ways. Colet was dean of St Paul's and chose to launch his assault in a sermon before the Canterbury Convocation in 1512. Identifying secularism, ambition, covetousness and immorality as the principal weaknesses, he declared, 'This reformation and restoring of the Church's estate must needs begin of you, our fathers, and so follow in us your priests in all your clergy'. More, a colleague of both Colet and Erasmus, chose to express his views in *Utopia* in 1516. In this fictional story, Utopia was a country where 'all priests are exceptionally pious, which means that there are very few of them'. Calls for reform were also apparent in Italy. Cardinals Sadoleto and Contarini urged Leo X to rid the Church of its corruption. In 1512 cardinal Giles asked rhetorically: 'When has the licence to sin been more shameless? ... When have the signs, portents, and prodigies both of a threatening heaven and of a terrified earth appeared more numerous or more horrible?' The Fifth Lateran Council, which opened in Rome that year, also recognised the need to raise standards of preaching, to insist that clerics 'live chastely and continently', and to stamp out 'the nefarious pest simony'.

In evaluating the complaints against the Church, real and imagined, it is clear that most were made by clergymen and academics, some by town councils, and a minority by lawyers and property owners. Some no doubt were made out of prejudice on account of the clergy's involvement in secular affairs; some were grievances against individual clerics or specific abuses; and some people, aware of the low quality of papal leadership and the lack of spiritual commitment of many bishops, justifiably expected a higher standard from the upper clergy and an improvement in the clergy below them. Yet in spite of the anti-clerical evidence which has survived and which has arguably attracted too much attention from historians in the past, the picture that has recently emerged is that the western Christian Church was not in such a poor condition as its critics claimed. Notably there was no widespread criticism of clerical teaching. Most accepted the Church for what it was: an institution that was far from perfect but indispensable in providing a path to heaven for their soul. But this state of affairs was not good enough for the reformers.

5 Evidence of Reform

> **KEY ISSUES** What examples of reform were there before 1517? Was a reformation inevitable?

a) The Regular and Secular Orders

The Catholic Church was not a static institution, incapable of change or unwilling to accommodate reform. It has already been noted that several monastic orders instituted stricter rules in the fifteenth century and, in Italy, Germany, France and Spain, monks were re-housed in 'congregations' of canons. Luther, for example, attended the Augustinian monastery of Erfurt which had been reformed as an Eremite order. Regular Dominican and Franciscan orders promoted many of the devotional manuals and there was a genuine attempt by some monks and friars to make themselves more relevant in a changing world. Some laymen performed social and charitable work but chose to live within the precincts of a monastery. The Oratory of Divine Love, for example, performed spiritual exercises, said prayers and worked with the poor and homeless in Genoa and Rome. Similarly, a small number of women in Germany and the Netherlands entered convents or formed their own 'beguine' house where they spent their day in prayer and poverty.

Mysticism, which originated at the end of the fourteenth century, was increasingly practised by both monastic orders and lay scholars. They believed that through prayer and meditation they could communicate directly with God. Although the Church was naturally suspicious of ideas that could by-pass the centrality of the sacraments and the pivotal role of the priest, works such as *The Imitation of Christ* and *The Book of Margery Kemp* proved hard to suppress. The fifteenth century also saw a new Dutch order of laymen and women known as the Brethren of the Common Life. They taught a form of spiritual piety called the 'devotio moderna' whereby spiritual perfection could be attained through prayer, meditation, chastity and poverty. By making the Bible and the life of Christ the basis of their belief, the 'devotio moderna' provided a refreshing alternative to the sterility of traditional ideas still being taught in most universities.

b) Lay Piety and Christian Humanism

The ideas of the Brethren spread quickly, particularly after 1450 when printing presses were set up across Europe. By 1500 there were 45 presses in France, 64 in Germany, 73 in Italy and four in England. Indeed the growth of literacy and the accompanying desire to acquire all kinds of religious literature goes a long way towards explaining the tremendous increase in lay piety and interest in the works of Christian humanists in the late fifteenth century. No single form of devotional work predominated. Thus, *The Imitation of Christ*, the best known mystical study, went through 99 editions before 1500. In England, the lives of saints recounted in the *Golden Legend*, and devotional works like *The Scale of Perfection* and *Mirror of the Blessed Lyfe of Jesu Crist*, proved very popular.

Of course, not everyone could read: indeed, it is likely that most people could not but they could still set their own agenda for spiritual renewal. Some devoted part of each day to prayer, a few had their own chapels and confessors and many endowed their parish church with cash and goods. As a result, spires were re-built, naves enlarged, side altars added and stained glass installed. Cathedrals were similarly endowed with chantry chapels, paintings, relics, ornaments, lamps and lights. All of this religious activity testifies to the diverse nature of popular piety during this period.

The fifteenth century also saw the development of Christian humanism. In the course of the Renaissance, classical ideas were studied and the concept that man could determine the truth for himself encouraged some scholars to examine the Scriptures more critically. Greek and Hebrew texts, it was believed, contained divine truths which once discovered would enable the Church to be restored to its pristine condition. The principal exponent of this view was Desiderius Erasmus, a Dutch scholar who had been educated at a Brethren school. He claimed that religion had become too mechanistic and conventional and, although it was not wrong to observe outward forms of devotion, it was more important to follow the teaching of Christ. In 1516 he revealed his finest humanist scholarship when he published the New Testament in Greek and Latin. His version provided a textual criticism and commentaries on the differences between the original Greek and the official Latin Bible, the Vulgate. And, of course, in pointing out the errors in the Vulgate, he was indirectly challenging orthodox beliefs. If this work was never intended to threaten the unity and universality of the Church, it certainly encouraged others to ask more searching questions and future reformers, such as Luther, Zwingli, Bucer and Calvin, all claimed to have been inspired by it.

Erasmus was just one of many humanists critical of the Church. Jacob Wimpfeling, professor of poetry at Heidelberg, was a stern critic of clerical abuses; Johannes Reuchlin, a Hebraist, published an edition of penitential psalms; and Johann von Staupitz, dean of the faculty of theology at Wittenberg university, condemned the popular appeal of indulgences. And many more preachers, poets, writers, printers and booksellers met the growing demand among literates and scholars for biblical texts and religious works.

Outside Germany, biblical humanism had less of an impact. In England, its activity was centred on the London Inns of Court, the two universities and the royal court. Prominent among the humanist reformers were Lady Margaret Beaufort (d.1509), who founded Christ's College, Cambridge, and patronised William Caxton, who printed mainly devotional works; John Fisher, who founded St John's College, Cambridge, and introduced Greek and Hebrew into its curriculum; John Colet, who began St Paul's school where he taught Greek; and Thomas More, writer, scholar, and lawyer, who befriended Erasmus. In their own way each contributed to humanist studies. A similar picture emerged in France. Jacques Lefèvre d'Etaples produced his own Latin edition of the Scriptures, which were later (in 1523) translated into French, and in 1512 published his commentaries on the Epistles of St Paul. At the court, Marguerite d'Angoulême, sister of Francis I, patronised humanist reformers like Guillaume Briçonnet, bishop of Meaux, who from 1515 began plans to reform his diocese.

In Spain, humanist studies made little progress due to the repressive influence of Salamanca university and to Queen Isabella and King Ferdinand, the Catholic Monarchs' orthodox Catholicism, but certain features of the Spanish church were reformed by cardinal Cisneros, Archbishop of Toledo (1495-1517). He wrote several devotional works, produced a new liturgy for the Castilian clergy and forced the secular clergy to reside in their parishes. Perhaps his best known contribution to church reform and to humanist studies was Alcalá university, which he founded to raise the quality of men entering the priesthood and which in 1517 produced the Polyglot – a translation of the Bible in parallel columns of Latin, Greek and Hebrew.

Some of the most radical social and religious developments occurred in Florence in the 1490s. The Observant Dominican prior, Girolamo Savonarola, preached that 'a mighty scourge' would soon cleanse the church in Italy and that Florence would become the New Jerusalem. Carried along by a mixture of popular hysteria, religious energy and messianic fervour, and the news that Italy had been invaded by a French army, he carried out far-reaching reforms. Blasphemers, adulterers and prostitutes were expelled or burned at the stake, and, in a society that had become over concerned with materialism, luxuries and vanities were condemned. His reform programme, however, was too rapid and revolutionary for most Florentines, who in 1498 took their revenge and executed him.

6 Conclusion

It is extremely difficult, if not impossible, to judge accurately the condition of the western Catholic Church. The historian's task is not helped by the fragmentary and, at times, biased nature of the surviving evidence, or by the large area which it covered. It is, however, clear from our examination of the Church over several decades that it was not sterile and inflexible but constantly changing. It had its faults and weaknesses, not least the spiritual aridity of monasticism and the amoral secularism of the Renaissance papacy, but the lower clergy struggled manfully to meet the needs of the people – and to a great extent appear to have been successful. Lay piety and Christian humanism demonstrated the strength of popular devotion and both the state and church had initiated reforms in the early sixteenth century. There was therefore no reason to think that the Church could not continue to evolve as it had in the past and accommodate itself to the lay and clerical changes. It seems likely that most people did not expect or want the Church to be reformed in 1517 and certainly not in the way that occurred.

Working on Chapter 2

If you have found the ideas expressed in this chapter difficult to understand, then do not worry. Although you may need to re-read it at a later stage in your course, you will be better served at this point by going on to the next chapter which you should find more straightforward. On the other hand, if you have understood much of the chapter and have an essay or exercise to complete based upon it, then you should give further thought to the ideas and examples. The questions in the issues boxes should be the start of your own line of thinking to ensure that you have followed the main arguments in each section. Since this chapter is concerned with differing views of the Church, you should think carefully about the issues and evidence presented before reaching your own conclusion. Do you, for example, think that a reformation was inevitable?

Answering structured questions on Chapter 2

Most AS and A-Level questions on this topic will test your understanding of either the condition of the Church or the attempts by reformers to change it before the Luther affair. For example, at AS you will probably have a two- or three-part structured question such as:

(a) Explain the main abuses in the Catholic Church at the beginning of the sixteenth century.
(b) How religious were people in western Europe during this period?

Examiners are looking for a number of clearly made points supported with accurate factual details, so it is important that you think carefully about your reasons and explanations in answering part (a). Although you may well be tempted to write a list of abuses, such as

24 The Condition of the Christian Church in Western Europe around 1517

nepotism, absenteeism, simony, biblical ignorance, immorality, or to generalise on the worldliness of popes, cardinals, monks and priests, it is important that you include in your answer factual examples and explanations of particular abuses.

Part (b) requires you to evaluate the extent to which people were content, critical or neutral, in their personal and public acts of worship. Some answers will be descriptions of popular religious practices but higher responses should attempt to assess the variety of religious activities in a range of countries and set them against the complaints of humanists and other reformers. You could take the reformers' desire to improve the spiritual condition of the Church as 'proof' that people were not very religious but this is not necessarily true. Indeed, you should seek to show that being 'religious' meant different things to different people. The majority had neither the ability nor desire to understand the finer points of Catholic theology but could relate to the concept of performing good deeds and participating in acts of atonement. Arguably, the most religious people were heretics because they were prepared to die for their beliefs. Do you agree?

Summary diagram
'The Condition of the Christian Church in Western Europe around 1517'.

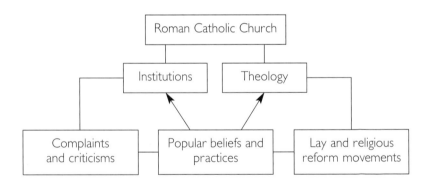

3 Martin Luther and the German Reformation

POINTS TO CONSIDER

The Reformation originated in Germany when Luther asked questions about the sale of indulgences. Before long, he was challenging the fundamental beliefs, institutions and authority of the Catholic Church. This chapter looks at the condition of Germany in 1517 and at Luther's theological ideas before considering why the 'Luther affair' had such a wide appeal in the 1520s.

KEY DATES

1517 Luther attacked the sale of indulgences in his *95 Theses*.
1518 Papal commission, headed by Cajetan, met Luther at Augsburg.
1519 Luther rejected papal authority in a debate with Eck at Leipzig.
1520 Luther wrote three pamphlets appealing to the German people.
1521 Leo X excommunicated Luther; the diet of Wörms imposed an imperial ban but Luther was protected by the elector of Saxony.
1522 Imperial knights adopted Lutheranism; Luther published the New Testament in German.
1524 Peasants' War began and spread to much of southern and western Germany.
1529 Five princes and 14 cities protested at not being allowed to practise Lutheranism; Luther disagreed with other reformers at Marburg over the meaning of the Eucharist.
1530 Confession of Augsburg defined Lutheran theology.
1534 Luther produced the first German Bible.
1546 Death of Luther.

1 Germany on the Eve of the Reformation

KEY ISSUE What was the condition of Germany around 1517?

a) Political Condition

The Holy Roman Empire was the largest political bloc of states in Europe, comprising more than 300 territories that stretched from the Netherlands in the west to Prussia in the east, from the Baltic in the north to the Swiss Alps in the south. Since 1437, the elected emperors had come from the Austrian Habsburg family, and they were in competition with other rulers for political supremacy in central Europe – with Scandinavian and Polish kings in the north-east and Baltic, with the Ottoman Turks in the south-east and with German princes like the Wettins of Saxony and Wittelsbachs of Bavaria in the Empire itself. Between 1493 and 1519, the Empire was ruled by Maximilian I. He was elected by the duke of Brandenburg, the king of Bohemia, the elector of Saxony, the count of the Palatinate, and the archbishops of Mainz, Cologne and Trier, electors who were in some respects more powerful than the emperor himself. They could raise a larger army, collect taxes from their subjects and control their state's judicial affairs. Machiavelli once observed that the crucial problem facing the emperor was that he had 'no power to enforce his will'. Attempts were made at various diets (assemblies) to establish a more centralised administration, regular taxation and a permanent army, but Maximilian lacked the skill and persistence to be successful and the estates had no desire to strengthen his power at their expense. Indeed, the territorial rulers claimed to have responsibility for their subjects' welfare, both temporal and religious, and clung tenaciously to their rights and privileges.

Saxony is a good example of the power struggle that was being played out by German states. In 1483 it had been divided into electoral and ducal territories which, in 1517, were held respectively by Frederick the Wise (1486–1525) and his cousin, George the Bearded (1500–39). Frederick was anxious to safeguard his lands from ducal Saxony, neighbouring Brandenburg and the Habsburg emperors, and, to this end, re-built his castle and established a university in the small town of Wittenberg. In 1502 he showed his readiness to stop papal indulgences from being sold in his lands when it became clear that the purpose of their sale – to raise money for a Turkish crusade – was not going to be achieved. Moreover, he had a substantial collection of relics and was keen to sell his own indulgences rather than those authorised by the pope.

The growing threat of the Turks to central and eastern Europe and, from a German perspective, to Austria and Hungary, should have instilled a sense of cooperation among princes but most rulers took the view that, unless the problem concerned them directly, they were disinclined to help the Habsburg emperor. More worrying to them was the lawless behaviour of many imperial knights, like Sickengen, Hutten and Cronberg, who attacked vulnerable towns and used their private armies to seize lands and goods. Franz von Sickengen, for example, preyed upon trade and shipping along the Rhine and held the city of Worms to ransom from 1514 to 1517. Only the formation of armed brigades, such as the Swabian League that operated in the south-west and was financed by local towns and princes, kept a semblance of order in the face of this knightly lawlessness.

Next to the princes the most important political force were the 65 imperial and free cities which were anxious to maintain their independence from the emperor and from neighbouring rulers. More than 80 per cent of the cities lay in the south of Germany and in the cantons of the Swiss Confederation which had broken free from imperial rule in 1499. Led by Nuremberg, Augsburg, Strasbourg and Ulm, each free city controlled a small group of local towns and surrounding villages (see the map on page 28). Ulm, for instance, dominated Memmingen, Biberach an der Riss, Kempten, Isny, and more than 50 villages. Considerable tension existed in most cities and towns between merchants and workers, nobles and servants, priests and parishioners, and this could be exploited by an ambitious prince, knight or bishop. Nuremberg, for example, was threatened by the Hohenzollern family, and Augsburg by the Wittelsbachs. Since the twelfth century, communal federations had been established in the Netherlands, south Germany and Switzerland, where royal authority was weak, and in the late fifteenth century these became leagues in which member states protected their communal rights. The Swiss Confederation became the model for cities, city-states and communities wishing to preserve their freedom, and political links established between south German and Swiss cities help explain why several German cities would 'turn Swiss' during the Reformation.

b) Religious and Cultural Conditions

We saw in Chapter 2 that Germany had a potent mix of anti-clericalism, anti-papalism and lay piety at the beginning of the sixteenth century. Anti-clericalism was not, in fact, particularly virulent: there had always been tales of lecherous monks, ignorant priests, absentee bishops and money-grabbing clerics; and medieval dramas such as *The Rise and Fall of Antichrist* and satires by Erasmus were highly popular (see page 19). In north Germany, few clerics had a university degree and the quality of sermons was poor; in the Lower Rhine, half of all benefices had absentee priests; and in the south, where there were several peasant uprisings, the rebel leaders generally held the clergy responsible for their urban and agricultural problems. Their complaints appear to have been justified. In Bavaria, for instance, peasants on ecclesiastical lands, unlike those under secular landlords, had annual tenancy agreements, which meant that rents could be and often were raised arbitrarily.

Anti-papalism was very strong for a number of reasons. Papal taxes, fees for licences and dispensations, and the curia's attempt to extend its control over ecclesiastical patronage, were all resented. So, too, was the appointment of Italian cardinals to German bishoprics; many remained in Italy or were regularly moved to a different diocese to enable the papacy to collect annates more frequently. Princes and imperial cities regularly complained in the German diets but, because there was no centralised authority to resist these practices, nothing was achieved.

An important trend in this period was the lay demand to reform abuses and achieve greater religious piety. Chantries, confraternities

Germany during the Reformation

and pilgrimages grew in popularity, people bought holy relics and indulgences, and the growth in the cult of the Virgin Mary and St Anne, all point to a revival of religiosity throughout the Empire. Several secular authorities tried to meet the demand and reform abuses: in the Palatinate, for example, all clerical appointments had to be approved by the elector, Nuremberg town officials supervised their church property and the appointment of preachers, and in Strasbourg limits were imposed on the amount of land that could be bequeathed to the Church. Travelling friars, pastors and preachers spread both traditional and new ideas, but the most popular works were biblical extracts, saints' lives and devotional books. Catechisms like Dietrich Kolde's *Mirror of a Christian Man* (printed in 1470) ran to 19 editions before 1517 and Erasmus's *Enchiridion Militis Christiani* (Handbook of a Christian Soldier) in 1503 established him as Germany's leading humanist. He revealed in print what many Germans had long felt – that religion had become full of conventions and rituals. He suggested that the only way to become a true Christian was to acquire a deeper understanding of the Scriptures and to study them in Hebrew, Greek and Latin.

The printing press popularised Erasmus's work. Germany and Switzerland had more than 70 presses by 1500 and led the way in publishing houses and distribution centres. Although the papacy granted Cologne university and the archbishop of Mainz the right to censor undesirable publications, the absence of any central authority in Germany meant that printers outside their jurisdiction could be easily found. Well might the German humanist Jakob Wimpfeling claim in 1515 that it was 'the noble art of printing which makes it possible to propagate the correct doctrines of faith and morals throughout the world and in all languages'. Erasmus would have agreed. In 1516 he produced a translation of the Greek New Testament, set it alongside the Latin version of the Vulgate, and added an extensive commentary on the classical sources and word derivations. By examining vital words and phrases, Erasmus was questioning orthodox beliefs. For instance, he translated 'do penance' as 'be penitent', which suggested Christ was concerned with inner attitudes rather than the sacrament of penance, and he showed that the Latin *sacramentum*, which was traditionally understood to mean the 'sign of a sacred act', actually meant a 'mystery' in Greek. Several theologians, including Luther, Zwingli and Calvin, drew inspiration from this work of biblical humanism.

The German historian Bernd Moeller once wrote: 'Humanists were not representative of German religious life in the latter years of the fifteenth century.'[1] While this remains true, since only a minority of Germans could read and even fewer wanted to study Greek and Hebrew, there had been a recent expansion in higher education and, with it, a quest for knowledge. The Italian Renaissance had spread ideas of *imperium* (political sovereignty) and civic virtue, and these appealed to nobles and town authorities, eager to acquire greater control of secular and religious institutions. The imperial knight, Ulrich von Hutten, for example, studied Tacitus's *Germania* and the chronicles of medieval rulers, and German lawyers like Lupold of Bebenburg and Conrad of Megenburg advanced the concept of *imperium*. Religious dramas, devotional literature, painting and church music may well have had a much greater popular cultural impact but we must not underestimate the role of humanism in shaping the ideas and attitudes of the leading theologians and political figures.

c) Social and Economic Conditions

The late fifteenth and early sixteenth century saw important economic and social developments in Germany that made a reformation of the Church more than likely. Firstly, a steady increase in population meant that Germany had more towns than anywhere else in Europe. Although the largest cities of Cologne (40,000) and Nuremberg (30,000) were less than half the size of Paris or Valencia, Germany had several cities in excess of 20,000 – Strasbourg, Augsburg and Ulm, for example – and the largest overall population in Europe. Most people still lived and worked in the countryside but the role of the 2,000 or so towns and cities in shaping the political and religious life of German society was a distinctive feature. The rise in population also put pressure on existing levels of agricultural production, and poor harvests caused food shortages, inflation and social distress for much of the 1510s.

Changes were also taking place in patterns of trade. Much of the trade between the Baltic and northern Europe had been controlled by the cities of the Hansa, a trade consortium, led by Cologne, Lübeck, Danzig and Hamburg, but by 1500 their monopoly was under threat from Danish and Dutch merchants. The south of Germany, on the other hand, saw an expansion in trade and industry. The export of fustian cloth to the emerging Antwerp market brought sizeable profits to the upland merchants, and new techniques in mining led to a boom in copper and silver mines centred on Saxony and Bohemia. As a result, Ulm, Augsburg and Nuremberg flourished as centres of arms manufacturing, and some individuals became rich. Jakob Fugger, for instance, an Augsburg banker, loaned money to mining speculators, exported silver and copper, and controlled much of the trade between Swabia and Antwerp. Luther's father also profited although on a much smaller scale. At first he worked in a copper mine but was later able to acquire the leasehold of several works and employed a small number of miners in Saxony.

Nobles, bishops and landlords, who were mainly dependent on fixed rents, saw their incomes decline, but it was the peasantry who most felt the impact of economic changes during this period. Landowners resisted attempts by peasants to end their feudal obligations or to have them converted to money payments; some landowners tried to raise rents or re-introduce feudal practices. Where serfdom persisted in much of northern and eastern Germany, the peasants were accustomed to harsh conditions, but in the south and south-west many had gained their freedom and were keen to remain tenant farmers. And it was in regions like Swabia and Franconia, where living standards had improved, that peasant uprisings were most frequent. The 'poor Conrad' revolt in Württemberg in 1514 was typical of these disturbances. Driven by a heady mixture of poverty and oppression, fired by sentiments that the world was about to end, and marching under the banner of a laced boot or *Bundschuh*, the peasants attacked lay and clerical landlords before being suppressed by troops from the Swabian League.

Recurrent famine, plague and violence were constant reminders of the fragility of life. As we have seen, the Church never let people forget the wages of sin and the ever-present threat of the Devil. Indeed, it was no coincidence that it was two Germans, Heinrich Kramer and Jakob Sprenger, who had acquired a papal bull in 1484 to hunt down witches. Their subsequent handbook of sorcery and witchcraft, the *Malleus Maleficarum*, which encouraged people to search for witches and remove anyone remotely associated with the forces of evil, added to the social instability of the age. Fear of death and the daily temptations of the Antichrist were concerns shared in varying degrees by all people who, in their hour of need, turned to the Church for guidance and comfort. One such person was Martin Luther.

2 Luther and the Catholic Church

KEY ISSUES What did Luther believe? How did he develop his theology?

MARTIN LUTHER

-Profile-

Born in 1483 to Hans Luther, a smelter-master, and Margaret, daughter of a well-to-do family, in Eisleben, Saxony. Educated in nearby Mansfeld and Magdeburg, Luther went to Erfurt university in 1501, where he gained a BA and then an MA. His father expected him to study for a law degree but a severe thunderstorm so frightened him that he vowed to enter an Observant Augustinian monastery in search of a merciful God. His tutor, Johannes von Staupitz, encouraged him to memorise the Bible – which he did. Ordained as a priest in 1507, he widened his theological studies, and became a visiting lecturer at Erfurt and Wittenberg universities. The monastic routine and a visit to Rome in 1511 failed to satisfy his search for salvation and he immersed himself in gaining his doctorate and then, between 1513–20, giving a series of university lectures as the professor of biblical studies at Wittenberg. It was during this period that he read (and re-read) the New Testament which changed his life and those around him forever. He agonised over whether man was born to suffer eternally as a result of the fall of Adam and the crucifixion. Was there nothing that Luther could do to assuage the pain of living and his fear of death apart from perform good works and buy indulgences? What gave the papacy the right to interpret the Bible? Was it possible that the pope was in league with the Devil or, worse, was the Antichrist? Such questions troubled Luther greatly as he developed and revised his ideas before arriving in the early 1520s at a more settled and mature theology.

a) Indulgences and Good Works

On 31 October 1517, Luther pinned 95 theses to the church door in Wittenberg and broadcast his intention to hold an academic debate on the subject of indulgences. He was appalled by the popularity of an itinerant indulgence-seller, Johann Tetzel, and felt that he had a responsibility to his fellow Germans to dissuade them from buying them. He explained his reasons in his theses, five of which are listed below.

Extracts from the 95 Theses[2]
20 The pope, by his plenary remission of 'all' penalties, only refers to those imposed by himself.
21 Hence the preachers of indulgences are wrong when they say that a person is absolved from every penalty by the pope's indulgences.
27 It is mere human talk to preach that the soul flies out [of purgatory] immediately the money jingles in the collection-box.
43 Christians need to be taught that those who give to the poor or lend to the needy do a better action than if they purchased pardons.
86 Why does not the pope, whose wealth is today greater than the riches of the richest, build just this one church of St Peter with his own money, rather than with the money of poor believers?

What had caused Luther to make this public outburst? He was convinced that neither Pope Leo X, nor Tetzel's employer, Albrecht, archbishop of Mainz, really appreciated how far the 'common people' had been misled by Tetzel's sales talk. In Luther's view, there was no biblical justification for the sale of indulgences and the time had come to expose this papal scam. From the time he went to university, and possibly earlier if we accept the view that he was influenced deeply by his father's mining culture and belief in the forces of evil, Luther was affected by a fear of death and the presence of the Devil. St Augustine's teachings of the certainty of death and human suffering, Bernard of Clairvaux's warnings of the power of the Antichrist, and Tauler's belief that Christianity could protect but not save a person from the temptations of evil, all left a powerful impression on young Luther. Indeed, as Heiko Oberman has said, 'Christ and the Devil were equally real to him: one was the perpetual intercessor for Christianity, the other a menace to mankind till the end.'[3] When Luther was a monk, endless prayers, spiritual exercises, spells of flagellation and fasting, all failed to appease his restless search for salvation. He first began to question the claim that indulgence sellers could remit sins when he was preparing for his lectures on the Psalms and Romans in 1513–15. 'The way I see it', he declared, 'the Gospel of St Matthew counts such perversions as the sale of indulgences among the signs of the Last Days.' Two years later, he returned to the theme when he heard about Albrecht's plenary indulgence. Although he knew that part of the profit went to Rome and part to Albrecht, what he did not know was that this was to pay off debts the archbishop owed to Rome. Thus, when Luther pinned his *95 Theses* to the cathedral door, the archbishop was unlikely to let the matter pass. And neither would Tetzel's Dominican order, the scholastically trained theologians from rival universities, or the papacy, which had authorised the sale.

Although Luther periodically returned to the question of indulgences, not until March 1520 did he publish his definitive views on outward forms of personal salvation. If we performed good works, he claimed, it was because we were already saved; the latter was not conditional upon the former. Indulgences, chantries, pilgrimages, holy relics and rituals were all 'worthless'. He regarded the orthodox doctrine of free will as irrelevant; indeed, it served as an impediment to achieving salvation because it encouraged people to put their trust in good works and not in faith alone. He declared: 'We ought first to know that there are no good works except those which God has commanded, even as there is no sin except that which God has forbidden. Therefore whoever wishes to know and to do good works needs nothing else than to know God's commandments.'[4] His publication *On Good Works* went through eight editions in seven months, and six more by 1525. Luther regarded it as his finest work.

b) Papal Authority: *Sola Scriptura*

In the course of 1518 and 1519, Luther had to defend his ideas in writing and in public debates. As he did so, he began to question the Treasury of Merits, the sanctity of saints and the existence of purgatory, until he found himself rejecting much of the penitential system and the papal authority which endorsed it. This was not something that Luther had desired or anticipated in 1517, but it occurred as he began to think more about his theology. As his principal adversaries, mainly Dominicans, pushed him into making more radical statements, so they unwittingly helped to clarify his thoughts. Early in 1518 Tetzel accused Luther of being a heretic, and Prierias, the pope's official theologian, defended the concept of papal infallibility. Luther replied in May by saying that popes were human and humans made mistakes. While he had nothing personal against Leo, he explained that the office of the papacy was subordinate to a general council of the Church and only it could rule on articles of faith. Cajetan, the imperial cardinal, met Luther at Augsburg in October. He was instructed by the pope to silence Luther but knew that nothing could be done without the consent of the elector, Frederick of Saxony, and the pope was counting on his support in stopping Charles Habsburg from becoming the next emperor. Not for the last time, international politics compromised the pope's perspective of the Luther affair. Cajetan was not prepared to debate Luther's theses but instead called upon him to admit he was in error. Luther's reply was predictable: he refused, claiming that Leo was a 'badly-informed pope who needed to be better informed'.

He was now well aware that he faced excommunication and that his life was in danger. His fate clearly rested with the elector, who was determined to stop the pope from interfering in what he believed was essentially a German affair. As a result, he refused to hand Luther over to Cajetan until he had had a fair hearing. Luther, of course, was still waiting to defend his position in an academic debate. In January 1519, the emperor died and papal attention moved from Luther to the imperial election but the Dominicans were not so willing to let matters stand still. Dr Eck, professor of theology at Ingolstadt, challenged Wittenberg university to a debate at Leipzig, a Dominican stronghold. Even before it began, Luther threw down the gauntlet by claiming that there was no biblical or historical evidence, nor canon law, to support the pope's claim to be head of the Church. Privately, Luther had concluded that the Antichrist had taken root in the papacy and that the only true authority was the Scriptures, a view which would be drawn out of him in the course of the debate. Wittenberg was represented by its head of department, Andreas Karlstadt, and by Luther and Melanchthon, but Eck quickly got the better of Karlstadt and taunted Luther by calling him a Hussite (see page 12). Luther, swept along by the occasion, claimed that Hus should never have been burned, that the council that condemned him had erred, and that popes had also made mistakes. In his opinion, only the Scriptures were beyond fallibility: *sola scriptura*. In defending himself in front of a biased audience and in a debate presided over by George, duke of Saxony, the elector's rival, Luther had publicly expressed more radical thoughts than he had intended and, in so doing, extended the charges against him.

In 1520 two publications came to his attention which proved that the papacy was a fraud. First, he read an edition of Valla's exposé of the *Donation of Constantine* which revealed that the transfer of power in the fourth century from the Roman emperor to the pope embodied in the donation was in fact a forgery. Second, he read Prierias' *Refutation* of 1519 that condemned Luther and confirmed papal infallibility. Both documents were lies, he felt, and proof that the Antichrist was at hand. 'The time for silence is over', he declared, 'the time to speak has come.' He had failed to win over the Church or to convince academics: now he had to persuade the German people – the future of Christianity rested with them, not with Rome. In June 1520 he wrote in German an *Address to the Christian Nobility of the German Nation*. He contended that three walls had been constructed around Rome and each was built on false foundations: first, that the pope's authority was superior to that of secular powers; second, that only the pope could interpret the Scriptures; and third, that only the pope could call a general council to reform the Church. He appealed to German nationalism, stating:

1 In name the Empire belongs to us, but in reality to the pope. We Germans are given a clear German lesson. Just as we thought we had achieved independence, we became the slaves of the craftiest of tyrants; we have the name, title, and coat of arms of the Empire, but the pope
5 has the wealth, power, the courts and the laws. Thus the pope devours the fruit and we play with the peels.[5]

In a substantial list of 27 points, Luther called for an end to payments and all appeals to Rome, demanded that German bishops should be appointed by the emperor and asked all secular rulers to press for a general council of the Church. It was Luther's first political commentary, and two more quickly followed. In *On the Babylonian Captivity of the Church* (August 1520), he claimed that the Church had been forced into a state of paganism by a Babylonish-styled papacy. Luther was now convinced that the pope was the Antichrist, a view he repeated in a treatise in October, *On Christian Freedom*. 'Is it not true that under this vast sky, nothing is more corrupt, more pestilential, more hateful than the Roman curia?', he asked. He did not wait for a reply. He was already in receipt of the papal bull, *Exsurge Domine*, that listed 41 errors in his teachings, and which gave him 60 days to recant or face excommunication. His response was to burn the bull in a public ceremony in Wittenberg on 10 December 1520, cheered on by university students and colleagues.

c) Justification by Faith Alone: *Sola Fide*

Luther's protest against indulgences and his stance on papal authority did not occur in isolation or in a coherent manner; they were part of his spiritual development which resulted from his ongoing lectures, sermons, private discussions and public debates. In his search for salvation, he had reacted against the scholastic authorities of Aristotle and Aquinas, found the writings of Scotus and Occam to be inadequate, and the ideas of mystics and humanists to be enlightening but not satisfying. Solace would be found in St Paul's *Epistle to the Romans*, which Luther first delivered to his students early in 1516.

Richard Marius, Luther's most recent biographer, has questioned how far Luther at this point had actually worked out his doctrine of *sola fide* (faith alone) and argues that it was not fully developed until late 1519. At Heidelberg in April 1518, when Luther first expounded his thoughts on salvation before a gathering of Augustinians, he revealed the beginning of his 'theology of the cross', by which God showed himself through Christ's suffering on the cross as the only true path to righteousness. At Augsburg in October, Luther had outlined how faith alone justified an individual in the eyes of Christ, and it is possible, as Marius claims, that he had his 'tower experience' during the autumn lectures. Certainly, it was not until October 1520 that he formally presented his doctrine of justification by faith alone in *On Christian Freedom*.

> 1   I shall set down the following two propositions concerning the freedom and the bondage of the spirit: A Christian is a perfectly free lord of all, subject to none. A Christian is a perfectly dutiful servant of all, subject to all ... One thing and only one thing is necessary for Christian life,
> 5   righteousness and freedom. That one thing is the most holy Word of God, the Gospel of Christ ... The Word of God cannot be received and

cherished by any works whatever, but only by faith. Therefore it is clear that, as the soul needs only the Word of God for its life and righteousness, so it is justified by faith alone and not by any works ... Yes, since
10 faith alone suffices for salvation, I need nothing except faith exercising the power and domination of its own liberty. This is the inestimable power and liberty of Christians.[6]

In 1517 Luther had been afraid of death; by 1520 he had found reassurance in the theology of the cross. It had not been the sudden revelation which some historians have claimed but a gradual process of self-examination before he discovered that his own suffering and that of Christ were identical experiences. At this point he was reluctant to elaborate upon the concept of predestination but he did so in 1525, when he defended his views on salvation and bitterly attacked Erasmus's *A Discourse On Free Will*. In Luther's opinion, expressed in *The Bondage of the Will*, man had no choice concerning his conduct when confronted with forces of goodness and evil; God alone decided his fate. All that he could do was to apply his life according to the Scriptures and put his trust in faith.

d) The Sacraments

Between 1519 and 1520 Luther expressed his views on the sacraments of the Church. In three sermons given in October and December 1519, he spoke about penance, baptism and the Eucharist, and for the first time questioned the validity of the remaining four sacraments. Having studied Erasmus's recent translation of the Greek New Testament and consulted his university colleagues, Luther was convinced that only three sacraments were to be found in the Scriptures: baptism, penance and the Eucharist (in 1522 he would argue that penance was also not vital). In August 1520, he expressed his ideas more fully in *On the Babylonian Captivity of the Church* by rejecting clerical celibacy, confirmation, the ordination of priests and the last rites, because, in his view, these sacraments were unknown at the time of Christ. He wrote:

1 I must deny that there are seven sacraments, and must lay it down, for the time being, that there are only three – baptism, penance and the bread – and that by the court of Rome all these have been brought into miserable bondage, and the Church despoiled of all her liberty ... Let
5 every man then who has learnt that he is a Christian recognise what he is, and be certain that we are all equally priests, that is that we have the same power in the word, and in any sacrament whatever, although it is not lawful for anyone to use this power, except with the consent of the community.[7]

By stressing the importance of baptism, he made redundant the idea that priests were in any way special. This was an idea that would revolutionise theological and political thinking. A corollary to the concepts of liberty and equality being grounded in Scripture was his interpretation of the Eucharist. He applied the logical step that both the bread and the wine at communion should be made available to the communicant. The Church declared the taking of wine to be an exclusive right of the priesthood, a practice Luther rejected because it was unscriptural. 'I conclude therefore', he said, 'that to deny both kinds to the laity is impious and oppressive, and it is not in the power of any angel, nor of any pope or council whatever to deny them ... Each person should be allowed a free choice in seeking and using the Sacrament, just as in the case of baptism and penance.'

It would take him several years to rationalise in his mind the doctrinal aspects of the Eucharist and, at this stage, he preferred to leave undefined what Christ had meant by *hoc est corpus meum*. In 1523 he denounced the views of radicals, such as Karlstadt and Zwingli, and explained his belief that Christ's body was really present at communion but Christ did not enter the communicant when bread and wine were consumed – a concept known as consubstantiation. This was his interpretation at Marburg in 1529, when he disputed with Zwingli, and it was enshrined in the Augsburg Confession of 1530, the summation of Lutheran theology.

Luther at the end of 1520 had come a long way in three years and there was no turning back. Called before the imperial diet at Worms in April 1521 to defend his theological views, he refused to compromise or recant. As he explained to Emperor Charles V: 'Unless I am convicted by Scripture and plain reason – I do not accept the authority of popes and councils, for they have contradicted each other – my conscience is captive to the Word of God. I cannot and will not recant anything, for to go against conscience is neither right nor safe. Here I stand. I can no other. God help me. Amen.'[8]

He was declared an outlaw by the emperor, excommunicated by the pope and censored by most universities, Luther's fate once again rested with his patron, the elector of Saxony. Frederick did not let him down. As Luther left Worms, a condemned man, he was kidnapped for his own protection and spirited away to a secluded castle at Wartburg in the far west of Saxony. Not for the last time, imperial politics had played a decisive hand in the future of the German Reformation.

3 Luther's Appeal

> **KEY ISSUE** Why did Luther's theological ideas attract so much interest and support in the 1520s?

a) Luther's Character and Style of Communication

Luther's attack on the Catholic Church and papacy found an immediate response among German people. Part of his appeal rested in the courage that he had shown in defying the pope, the emperor and the Antichrist. This struck a chord with German nationalists like Franz von Sickingen and Ulrich von Hutten. 'After all', declared Hutten, 'it is not a question of Luther but of everyone; the sword is not raised against this one man alone, we are all of us under attack.'[9] Hutten was a humanist, who had assumed (wrongly) that Luther was as well, and saw him as a comrade-in-arms, a champion of German culture and liberty, protesting against scholasticism, Latinism, and all things Roman Catholic.

To many Luther was a national hero – a peasant, a saint, a prophet. It was an image which his supporters did much to publicise in the early 1520s through paintings, engravings and pamphlets. Luther related easily to the ordinary German. His lively and colloquial style, his ability to reach out and touch the common man, indeed helps to explain the popularity of his ideas. His language was at times earthy and urbane, often crude but frequently compelling, especially when he related his encounters with the Devil. He recalled in his Table Talk: 'When I awoke last night, the Devil came and wanted to debate with me; he rebuked and reproached me, arguing that I was a sinner. To this I replied: Tell me something new, Devil!'[10] Luther certainly knew how to tell a good story.

In spite of the imperial ban, Luther continued to lecture at Wittenberg, becoming dean of the theology faculty, and produced a rich variety of liturgical works ranging from the first German translation of the New Testament (1522) and a German Bible (1534), to catechisms, hymns, service books, and commentaries on the Lord's Prayer and Ten Commandments. During his lifetime, his writings went through nearly 4,000 editions, and the New Testament alone sold more than 200,000 copies in twelve years. It seems clear that without the printing press, Luther's theological ideas and clashes with authority would have been known only by a small number of people. When he appealed to church doctrine, he was able to cite specific biblical references which his audience could later read and judge for themselves. The Scriptures were thus revealed as printed words and in German; they required no sacred mediation and were accessible to all believers. In his view, the printing press was 'God's highest and extremest act of grace whereby the business of the Gospel is driven forward'. German presses and the workshops of publishing firms soon became religious, cultural and commercial centres where printer, scholar, engraver and merchant collaborated. Luther worked closely with artists like Lucas Cranach at the press of Hans Lufft in Wittenberg to produce illustrated publications for his semi-literate audience.

It should not be forgotten, however, that Luther was principally a preacher, for whom the sermon remained the prime means of communication. Between 1521 and his death in 1546, he preached more than 2,000 sermons, most of which were published in German, and addressed the issues of everyday life – baptism, marriage, communion and death. Evangelical preachers, who were educated at Wittenberg and went on to spread the 'word' throughout Germany, played a vital part in the Lutheran reformation. Osiander in Nuremberg, Zwilling in Torgau and Bugenhagen in Lübeck and Bremen, were three of many graduates that were invited by towns to preach 'nothing but the Gospel'. The appeal of Lutheranism lay very much in the way the spoken word was able to capture, hold and convert an audience.

b) Lutheran Theology

Luther's theological ideas were not always easy to follow or logically explained but the underlying principles were not difficult to grasp. His stance against the papacy, for instance, was understood and endorsed by many Germans. Some of them revealed their feelings of anti-clericalism and anti-papalism through acts of iconoclasm and violence against the monastic and parish clergy, and justified their actions as the will of God. Similarly, Luther's doctrine of the priesthood of all believers, *sola fide* and *sola scriptura*, certainly unleashed latent forces of liberty and equality. By encouraging every believer to think that they had the right to do whatever they desired, the very fabric of society was put at risk. Luther, of course, had not intended releasing such a genie and he was quick to condemn disorder in the name of the Gospel but 'Godly Law' undoubtedly had a widespread appeal.

Religious beliefs and political ambitions went hand in hand, and the established authorities soon realised how Lutheranism could help them. The imperial knights, anxious to halt their political decline, adopted Luther's ideas and besieged episcopal estates at Bamberg and Wurzburg in 1522, only to be defeated in battle by rival princes. A small number of princes, led by Albrecht of Hohenzollern, Philip of Hesse and John of Saxony, committed themselves to Lutheranism by 1526. Some were motivated by a genuine desire to eliminate clerical corruption and assumed the role of 'bishops' to implement reform. Others were attracted by the prospect of gaining control of church property and patronage, and of transferring papal taxation to their own pockets. And some, concerned at the attendant violence which threatened to sweep across Germany in 1525, were drawn by Luther's insistence on order and obedience. In 1529, just five princes signed the 'Protestation' that objected to the imperial decree banning their Lutheran practices, but this number would increase to 20 by 1546.

The historian Peter Blickle has stressed the importance of rural support for Lutheranism, at least in the early 1520s. Peasants, miners and weavers were attracted by Luther's appeal to Godly Law and the apparent egalitarianism of his assertion that 'we are all one body'. Luther was thinking in terms of spiritual equality but rising taxation had combined with bad harvests in 1523–24 to create widespread distress in the German countryside, and the belief that Luther was a messiah sent to redress popular grievances gave his theology a cutting edge. Hailed as a prophet, this was one of the factors behind the Peasants' War of 1524–6, a series of revolts which began in the Black Forest and affected most areas of Germany. But Luther had an innate repulsion of disorder – it was a sign of the Antichrist – and condemned the uprising in *Against the Robbing and Murdering Hordes of Peasants* (May 1525). His denunciation and the peasants' military defeat by the princes saw much of the idealistic gloss surrounding Lutheranism evaporate and goes a long way towards explaining why the movement became less popular in rural Germany in the following years.

Modern historians have attached increasing importance to Luther's appeal to the imperial cities and town councils. By 1546 most of the 65 free cities and hundreds of smaller towns had adopted Lutheranism. Recent studies have shown that each urban group responded to Luther's theology with individuality and diversity. At Wittenberg and Erfurt, the role of preachers was vital in stimulating and controlling the pace and extent of reform; at Nuremberg and Ulm, the city councils implemented changes but only after a public debate and vote had been taken; and in Strasbourg, the town guilds played a decisive part in introducing evangelical reforms.

c) Three Case Studies: Wittenberg, Nuremberg and Strasbourg

Wittenberg experienced rising tension in the early 1520s from a variety of quarters. Students and academics threatened the Catholic clergy if they did not introduce changes and the arrival of visionary prophets from nearby Zwickau led to an outburst of iconoclasm in 1521–2. Luther was aware of the elector's concern at the growing disorder and called for a slow, disciplined reformation, that preserved rather than destroyed the past. The town council agreed. Once order had been restored, changes re-commenced with baptisms (1523), hymns (1524) and finally masses (1525), conducted in the vernacular. When Luther published a liturgy in the following year, it combined traditional rituals (such as the elevation of the host) with novel practices (German prayers). The accession of a new elector in 1525 saw reforms gather pace as visitations were completed (1527–8) and educational and social programmes developed by Luther for the whole of Saxony.

The imperial city of Nuremberg found itself in a difficult position in the 1520s. It had a strong humanist tradition, was a centre of printing (Dürer worked there) and was keen to introduce Lutheran reforms. Indeed, its two pastors in 1521, Andreas Osiander and Dominicus Schleupner, were allowed by the council to spread

Luther's ideas so long as they did not cause disorder. By 1524 communion was being celebrated in both kinds, baptism was conducted in German and a common chest had been set up for the poor. Nuremberg was indeed ahead of Wittenberg but it was acutely aware that the emperor would not take kindly to a reformation. Nuremberg was a large, prosperous city, which held three diets between 1522 and 1524, and was the permanent seat of imperial justice. Caution was the keynote in the council as its members tried to weave a passage between upholding the *Reichstag* decree against Luther, conform to the Scriptures and retain order in the city. The turning-point was reached in March 1525 when a debate was held in the city hall between orthodox and reform groups. Osiander presented a good case in favour of substantial changes along Lutheran lines and when the result was announced by the city's legal adviser, Christopher Scheurl, who chaired the meeting and was known to favour reform, the crowd outside the building cheered their approval. Only then did the council permit reforms to begin: the bishop's authority was suspended, monasteries were closed and the mass was abolished. It took some time to replace the Catholic members of the council but by 1528 there was enough support to establish a church ordinance that laid down the ecclesiastical laws governing the city and its rural parishes. The city was undeniably Lutheran – in 1529 it was one of the 14 cities that signed the 'protestation' – and, whatever the evangelical motives of the leading councillors, its reformation had been accomplished constitutionally. Nevertheless, the councillors felt it was prudent to maintain Catholic links outside the city and be as conciliatory as their consciences would allow in their dealings with the emperor.

Unlike most German cities, Strasbourg tolerated a variety of faiths and, for much of the sixteenth century, was regarded as a centre for religious exiles. Situated on the Upper Rhine, it had well-established trade links with France, Switzerland and southern Germany and was acknowledged as a leading centre for humanism. Its guilds played a prominent part in local politics and it was through the pressure of urban workers that the city council agreed in 1523 to appoint three evangelical preachers, Martin Bucer, Wolfgang Capito and Caspar Hedio, to join the cathedral priest, Matthew Zell. By 1524, all four preachers were calling for reforms, but the council was divided between one group which favoured no change; a second which welcomed Lutheran reforms; and a third that supported Zwinglianism. The council, concerned to maintain order in the city, insisted that the preachers 'confined themselves to Scripture'; but images and ornaments in churches started to be removed, wine was offered to the laity and baptisms and masses were said in German. Catholic services continued to be said until 1529 when the Latin mass was finally abandoned and monasteries were closed, yet the council was not willing to close its doors on a future reconciliation with the Catholic camp. Indeed, under the direction of Bucer, the city not only tried to unify

Lutherans and Zwinglians but to accommodate Anabaptists as well. The reformation in Strasbourg was unlike that in any other German city. Its Church Orders, introduced by Bucer between 1530 and 1534, modified mainstream Protestant views on justification and predestination; its theological position was more Zwinglian than Lutheran although Bucer was unwilling to subscribe to either Luther's or Zwingli's views on the Eucharist, and in 1530 he produced his own *Confessio Tetrapolitana*, which Strasbourg shared with Constance, Lindau and Memmingen. Pastors, teachers, deacons and elders were appointed to improve educational and pastoral care but his attempt to put discipline in the hands of the church elders was rejected by the council. In 1536 Strasbourg, fearful of being politically isolated following the collapse of Zwinglianism in Switzerland (see Chapter 4), threw in its lot with the Lutherans and negotiated the 'Wittenberg accord', but it still operated a policy of toleration towards most Protestant groups. One such beneficiary was John Calvin who arrived in 1538 to be the pastor of French exiles and before long another faith was being practised in the city. Not until 1598 did the council vote for Lutheranism to be the city's sole faith.

d) Conclusion

German people became Lutheran for a variety of reasons. Some did so for political motives to enhance their power as secular rulers and as members of a town council; some were motivated by financial considerations and wished to secularise church property and divert its wealth into the pockets of the laity. Others wanted to take education and poor relief out of the hands of the Church and establish a more effective system (see Chapter 7). Some believed that the state should assume greater responsibility for the moral and religious guidance of the people and welcomed the authoritarian character of the church ordinances. Perhaps, for most people, the deciding factor in their conversion to Lutheranism was the evangelical appeal which gave each person the prospect of salvation in a form that they could understand, afford and attain. That some read far more into Luther's theology than he ever intended, or reduced many of his complex ideas into over-simplifications, is hardly surprising given the climate of expectation, discontent and enthusiasm that greeted his ideas in Germany.

Footnotes

1. B. Moeller, 'Religious Life in Germany on the eve of the Reformation' in G. Strauss (ed.), *Pre-Reformation Germany* (Macmillan,1972), p. 27.
2. *Martin Luthers Werke. Kritische Gesamtausgabe* (Weimar,1883), vol 1, pp. 233–5.
3. H. Oberman, *Luther: Man Between God and the Devil* (Yale U.P.,1989), p.104.

4. *Luthers Werke*, 6, pp.196–276.
5. *Ibid*, 6, pp. 463–4.
6. *Ibid*, 31, pp. 344–6.
7. *Ibid*, 6, pp. 497–573.
8. H. J. Hillerbrand, *The Reformation in its Own Words* (London,1964), p. 91.
9. E. Böcking (ed), *Ulrich von Hutten Schriften* (Leipzig,1861), 5, p. 302.
10. *Luthers Werke*, 6, p. 215.

Structured questions on Chapter 3

Consider the following typical AS questions:

(a) What were Luther's main criticisms of the Catholic Church between 1517 and 1520? *(10 marks)*
(b) Why was neither the Church nor the Emperor able to silence Luther? *(15 marks)*
(c) How do you account for the appeal of Luther in Germany? *(25 marks)*

Answering source-based questions on Chapter 3

Study the extracts on pages 32, 34, 35 and 36, and answer the following questions:

(a) Explain the meaning of 'the soul flies out of purgatory immediately the money jingles in the collection-box' (page 32). *(10 marks)*
(b) How useful is the extract from the *Address to the Christian Nobility* (page 34) as evidence of Luther's views on the papacy? *(25 marks)*
(c) How far does the extract *On Christian Freedom* (page 35–6) support or contradict the ideas expressed in the extract on page 36? *(25 marks)*
(d) On the basis of all of the extracts in this chapter and your own knowledge, do you think Luther was a conservative or a revolutionary leader? *(60 marks)*

The following points offer advice on how to answer these AS documentary questions:

(a) The principal instruction is to 'explain' and you must therefore do more than describe or comment on the words in the extract. The theological concept of 'purgatory' and the orthodox teaching that everyone's soul would have to be purged before it could pass to heaven needs to be explained, as well as the popular practice that was encouraged by the Church of paying for an indulgence. Supply your own factual knowledge so that the meaning of the passage is fully explained in its historical context.
(b) The extract is useful on two main counts: one, its content; and two, the nature of the document. The content is consistent with Luther's earlier comments about the authority of the pope, the wealth of the Church and the subjection of German affairs to Rome. However, unlike previous

open statements that had treated Leo with grace and goodwill, now the gloves were off and Luther's style was altogether more aggressive. Discuss Luther's appeal in German to the national interest against the background of his own impending doom. Comment also on the two later publications of 1520 which broadened his attack on the papacy.

(c) Comparative questions are best answered by assessing both extracts point by point. Consider how much of the passage on page 35 agrees with that on page 36. Points of difference as well as similarity need to be explained. Wherever possible, you should demonstrate your knowledge of events at the time in support of your answer. Do not spend valuable time quoting at length from the documents; instead, refer to particular phrases in your comparison.

(d) Read the extracts again and assess their general completeness as a set using your contextual knowledge to reach a conclusion. Indicate what the documents do not reveal or what extra knowledge is required for you to decide between 'conservative' and 'revolutionary' leader. In any documentary exercise, try to maintain a good balance between textual analysis and your own knowledge. This is not an essay question and marks will be lost if you treat it as one.

Summary diagram
'Martin Luther and the German Reformation'

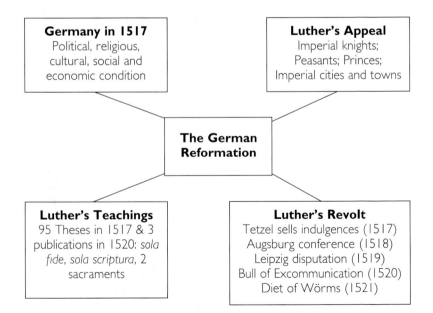

4 Zwinglianism, Radicalism and Calvinism

POINTS TO CONSIDER

This chapter looks at the other leading continental Protestant reformers and compares their ideas with those of Luther. It examines Zwinglianism, radicalism and Calvinism and asks, how did they evolve? What were their distinguishing features as reform movements and why were there different forms of Protestantism?

KEY DATES

1519 Zwingli began preaching in Zurich cathedral.
1521 The Prophets of Zwickau arrived in Wittenberg.
1523 Zurich council debated and accepted Zwingli's *67 Theses*.
1525 Swiss Brethren expelled from Zurich.
1529 Zwingli, Luther and Melanchthon met at Marburg; civil war began in Switzerland between Zwinglians and Catholics.
1531 Zwingli died at the battle of Kappel; civil war ended.
1535 Anabaptist city of Münster overthrown.
1536 Calvin published the *Institutes of the Christian Religion*.
1541 Calvin published the *Ecclesiastical Ordinances of Geneva*.
1549 Zurich Accord – Zwinglians and Calvinists formed the Swiss Reformed Church.
1559 Calvinist Academy opened in Geneva.
1564 Death of Calvin.

1 Zwingli and the Swiss Reformation

KEY ISSUES What were Zwingli's main beliefs? How, and with what consequences, were his ideas applied in Zurich, Berne and Basle?

ZWINGLI

Born in 1484, the son of a wealthy farmer, Ulrich Zwingli first studied at Vienna and then Basle universities, excelling in Latin and theology. Following his ordination in 1506 at Constance, he became parish priest of Glarus, where he stayed for ten years. There, he studied classical authors, taught himself Greek and Hebrew, and read as much as he could about German and Swiss

-*Profile*-

> humanism. He was particularly drawn to Erasmus's ideas and, like him, began to develop pacifist tendencies which brought him into conflict with his town council. Switzerland was renowned for its mercenaries – Zwingli twice accompanied troops to Italy as an army chaplain – but his experience at the battle of Marignano in 1515 led him to renounce warfare. Not surprisingly, his views were unwelcome and he moved to Einsiedeln and then to Zurich as a stipendiary priest in December 1518. By then, he had read Erasmus's Greek translation of the New Testament and was able to compare it with Jerome's fifth century Latin text. On 2 January 1519, Zwingli delivered his first sermon in the Great Minster at Zurich.

a) Zwingli's Theological Ideas

The most important influences upon his theology were the humanist ideas of Erasmus and the social and political condition of Zurich, where Zwingli lived and worked for more than 12 years. Though he and Luther held similar opinions concerning the need to reform the Catholic Church, Zwingli does not seem to have read any of Luther's works before 1519 and, in later years, consistently denied that he owed anything to the German theologian. Zwingli certainly stressed the significance of the Bible far more than Luther. He preached the Gospels in biblical order, beginning with *Matthew* and continuing to the end of the New Testament, before progressing to the Old Testament. In the course of 1519 he spoke out on a number of issues, condemning indulgences, the worshipping of saints and images, and the sterility of scholasticism. In 1520 he renounced his annual papal pension of 50 gulden, and felt free in his sermons to attack the materialist ambitions of the papacy. Indeed, in these early years, Zwingli's public addresses attracted large crowds as he explored social and moral issues.

Church reform began in 1522 when Zwingli challenged two traditional practices: fasting during Lent and clerical celibacy. In his *On the Choice and Freedom of Foods*, he argued that there was nothing in the New Testament about abstinence and each Christian should be allowed a free choice to decide for himself. Although he continued to fast, he was in the company of friends who ate sausages in Lent. Similarly, he claimed that there was no biblical justification that prevented priests from marrying. In fact, clerical celibacy was widely ignored in Switzerland and Zwingli himself was secretly married in 1522. Throughout the year, he was in correspondence with the bishop of Constance, who criticised his evangelical practices, but Zwingli had the support of the city council, and this proved vital. In October it re-confirmed his appointment as preacher and, when he resigned his post as a stipendiary priest, it was clear to whom he owed his authority. Indeed, it was the council that agreed to hold a public debate in January 1523 to hear the arguments for and against his beliefs. Zwingli set out his ideas in the *67 Theses* before some 600 spectators in the town hall. The bishop refused to attend – he had no wish to debate theological issues in German in front of a lay audience – and sent instead Johannes Fabri, who was simply no match for Zwingli.

Much of Zwingli's theology is contained in these theses – his belief in *sola fide* (by faith alone), predestination, *sola scriptura* (only the Bible), baptism and communion as the only valid sacraments, vernacular services, and married priests; and his denunciation of papal authority, the mass, transubstantiation, and monasteries. In each of these ideas, he agreed with Luther. However, there were significant differences too. Zwingli placed greater emphasis on *sola scriptura* than on *sola fide*, and insisted on preaching from the New Testament first. In fact, his biblicism was altogether more radical than Luther's – as he also rejected church images, music, fasting and the payment of tithes. Above all, he disagreed with Luther over the meaning of the Eucharist. To Zwingli, Christ's words 'This is my body' indicated that the mass was a commemorative act, that His body and blood were present at communion though only symbolically, and that the physical body of Christ was in heaven and not in the sacraments. Instead of celebrating the mass at an altar, he delivered the bread and wine from a table in the middle of the congregation as part of a commemorative meal. As he explained in Point 18 of his theses, 'Christ, having sacrificed himself once and for all, is for all eternity a perpetual and acceptable offering for the sins of all believers, from which it follows that the mass is not a sacrifice, but is a commemoration of the sacrifice of the salvation which Christ has given us'.[1] Luther disagreed. To him, Christ was both in spirit and in body everywhere, and he dubbed Zwingli a 'sacramentarian', someone who denied the sacraments. This was not strictly true, of course, but the more Zwingli objected, the more his opponents used it as a term of abuse. In 1529, when Luther and Zwingli met at the colloquy of Marburg for the first and only time, they agreed on 14 out of 15 articles of faith, but not on their interpretation of the Lord's Supper. In spite of the best efforts of Bucer, Capito and Melanchthon to reach a consensus, personal animosity tinged with pride underscored this theological difference, and the two leading European Protestant faiths went their separate ways.

b) Zurich and the Swiss Reformation (see the map on page 48)

In 1519 Zurich was one of 13 cantons in the Swiss Confederation which, 20 years earlier, had effectively won its political freedom from the emperor. Nominally within the diocese of Constance, the city was

48 Zwinglianism, Radicalism and Calvinism

The Empire, Switzerland and the Netherlands, 1517–1550.

really ruled by a council of 212 wealthy landowners, merchants and craftsmen. Each of the cantons was keen to preserve its autonomy and to protect its communal interests. Unlike Wittenberg, which was subject to its electoral prince, Zurich was answerable to its 6,000 or so citizens, and to its elected councillors. The city fathers were responsible for religious affairs, held the patronage of the major churches and had no intention of letting the bishop of Constance interfere in their reformation. And, in 1519, there was a general belief that the Church needed reforming. There was resentment at clerical privileges, corruption among many of the 200 priests in the city, dissatisfaction with the mechanical performance of Catholic rituals, and criticism of clerical taxation. The council, however, contained many who were reluctant or unwilling to introduce changes to the Church, and no one wished to incur the wrath of the emperor or the pope on account of Zwingli's innovations. Yet the council believed that it had a duty to meet the spiritual needs of its citizens and, provided the proposed reforms were implemented democratically and in an orderly fashion, it was willing to back Zwingli. Every aspect of church and government reform was therefore first discussed and debated in council meetings and synods, and, inevitably, progress was slow. Indeed, several years were to pass before Zurich became a totally Protestant city.

Immediately following Zwingli's successful defence of his ideas in January 1523, the council confirmed that 'all people's priests, pastors and preachers in the city, jurisdictions and territories, shall undertake to preach nothing but what can be proved by the holy Gospel and the pure holy Scripture', but there was resistance to this evangelicalism from the older Catholic families. Only in 1524 was fasting ended, images and crucifixes in churches removed, chantries and monasteries closed, and the clergy told to wear civilian clothes. Finally, in April 1525, the mass was abandoned but only then as an experiment for one year. In fact, it was not restored, and Zurich became a reformed city.

Zwingli's application of scriptural authority was also apparent in his attempts to reform the moral, social and educational condition of the people. In this respect, he again differed from Luther, who at first was principally concerned with the salvation of the individual. Zwingli and the council, on the other hand, believed the state had a duty to look after the interests of the community and uphold both secular and clerical standards, and this meant assuming those roles previously performed by the Catholic Church. Thus, in 1523 the council decreed that 'learned, skilful and upright men shall lecture on, and expound, the Bible publically every day' and 'schoolmasters, better paid than previously, shall be provided to be an active teacher and leader to the boys'. In 1525, the clergy was ordered to attend 'prophesyings' every weekday morning in the Great Minster. At these Bible meetings, a scholar lectured on the Scriptures in Latin, Greek and Hebrew, and the details were then explained in German to the audience. A system of poor relief was also established and four men were appointed to distribute alms to the poor and to those in hospital. The closure of monasteries and, in several cases, the voluntary surrender of title deeds to the city, provided funds to establish a common chest in 1525. Marital law courts were also set up to resolve disputes and enact divorce proceedings, and standards of behaviour were monitored from 1526 by a Court of Public Morals. The city council even had the power to excommunicate a citizen and, from 1526, to pass the death sentence for heresy.

The success of Zwinglianism owed much to Zwingli's belief that religion must be subject to the state. The threat of peasant revolts spreading to Switzerland from Germany, and the presence of Anabaptists in Zurich from 1523 (see page 54), led to the council seeking political support from nearby cantons. In 1527 Constance formed an alliance with Zurich, and in 1529 Glarus, Schaffhausen, Appenzell, Berne and Basle joined them in the Christian Civic Union. A handful of south German towns, such as Ulm, Memmingen, Augsburg and Frankfurt-am-Main, had also become members, partly attracted by Zwingli's theology and partly by their long-standing cultural and economic links with the Swiss towns. As Zwinglianism spread, so opposition arose principally from the Catholic Swiss cantons of Fribourg, Zug, Lucerne, Schwyz, Uri and Unterwalden. They were anxious not to be overrun by Zurich or to succumb to its Protestant beliefs, and they had the moral support of archduke Ferdinand of Austria, the emperor's brother, which gave them added strength. In 1529 they formed the Christian Alliance, and both sides prepared for war.

Zurich was particularly bullish and only the intervention of Berne, that called for a cease-fire after two days of fighting, prevented a bloodbath. However, fighting broke out again in 1531 and responsibility lay squarely with Zwingli and Zurich. His influence appears to have been in decline – he had failed to resolve his differences with Luther at Marburg (1529), he was absent from the Protestant conference at Augsburg (1530) and he was aware of the limited impact his reforms were having outside the Swiss cities. Zurich, for its part, wanted to expand its control into the inner rural and eastern cantons and unwisely imposed an economic blockade on them in an attempt to convert or crush Catholic opposition. In trying to accomplish a decisive victory, Zwingli and Zurich risked everything – and lost! At the battle of Kappel, Catholic troops caught the Protestants by surprise and Zwingli was among 500 killed in the fighting. By the ensuing peace treaty, Switzerland was divided into Catholic and Zwinglian cantons, each of which was free to decide its faith. However, Protestants were not tolerated in the eight Catholic cantons though Catholics were permitted to remain in the five Zwinglian states. Heinrich Bullinger was appointed Zwingli's successor and did his best to keep Zwinglianism alive in the face of competing faiths.

Nevertheless, his rivalry with Luther prevented any union with German Protestants, and the declining political significance of Zurich, combined with the rising power of Geneva and Calvin (see page 58), saw Bullinger and Calvin unite the Protestant Swiss churches into a Calvinist Reformed Church in 1549.

c) Two Case Studies: Berne and Basle

Berne was a small city in western Switzerland with a large rural population under its control. Surrounded by powerful Catholic cantons and anxious to preserve its independence from its traditional overlords, the duke of Savoy and the bishop of Basle, the city council adopted Protestant reforms with extreme prudence. It had received Lutheran literature in 1522 and, influenced by evangelical preachers Berchtold Haller and George Brunner, it agreed in 1523 that only sermons based on the Bible would be permitted. Significant changes occurred in 1525 – indulgences, tithes and clerical privileges were abolished, and the council assumed responsibility for clerical appointments – but there was strong resistance in rural areas. Gradually, however, a reform group won control of the Great Council and, in a public debate in January 1528, consent was gained to introduce thoroughgoing reforms for the entire canton. Zwingli, Bucer, Bullinger and Oecolampadius were in the audience and supported Haller. As a result, the mass was abolished, priests were allowed to marry, altars and images were removed, and church property was seized. In 1528 Berne became a Zwinglian state.

The city of Basle lay in the north of Switzerland and had a strong humanist tradition. Erasmus had had many of his works printed there and one of the scholars who assisted him in the translation of the Greek New Testament, Johannes Oecolampadius, became professor of theology at the university and was responsible for the city's subsequent reformation. Oecolampadius was in contact with Zwingli from 1522 and, although he shared many of Zwingli's ideas – he ate a suckling pig during Lent, for instance – his theology differed in a number of respects. He put more emphasis on the real presence of Christ at the Eucharist and he believed that church officers not civil authorities should be responsible for enforcing discipline in the city. As in the other Swiss and south German cities, the council set the pace and extent of reform. Until 1528, it generally supported the sermons of Oecolampadius but was reluctant to risk compromising political harmony in the name of religion. A period of intense popular pressure over the winter of 1528/29 changed its mind. Two churches were stripped of their Catholic ornaments, images elsewhere were ceremonially smashed, and anti-Catholic pamphlets, most probably orchestrated by the militant weavers' guild, forced the council to take action. In 1529 it agreed to abandon the mass and assumed responsibility for education and the poor. In the following year, it handed responsibility for pastoral and civil discipline to the lay elders. As in Zurich and Berne, Basle's reformation had been slow in the making but speedy in its execution.

2 Radical Sects: the Anabaptists

> **KEY ISSUES** What were the main beliefs of the radicals? How did various groups differ in their ideas? What was unique about the Anabaptists of Münster in the 1530s?

a) The Main Beliefs of the Radical Sects

No sooner had evangelical preachers revealed that the Bible held the key to salvation than all kinds of people began to develop their own interpretations. Believing that they were the true believers and that they had a God-given duty to spread the Word, many were anxious to introduce reforms as quickly as possible since an unreformed Church pleased the Antichrist and put their souls in peril. As a result, the 1520s saw numerous self-appointed 'prophets' emerge in Germany, Switzerland and the Netherlands.

These radical reformers did not pursue a common programme of reform; indeed, at no time was radicalism a united movement. However, in 1527 several south German and Swiss sects expressed in the Schleitheim Confession a number of beliefs which were shared by most radical groups. First, they rejected child baptism since Christ was baptised as an adult and there was nothing in the Bible to condone it. As a result, all radical groups were known as 'Anabaptists' because their members were re-baptised as adults. Second, anyone who committed a sin was banned or excommunicated. Third, they believed that holy communion should be made available to anyone who had already been baptised. Fourth, followers had to be ready for 'separation from the abomination'. As this article explained:

> 1 By this is meant all Catholic and Protestant works and church services, meetings and church attendance, drinking houses, civic affairs, the oaths sworn in unbelief and other things of that kind, which are highly regarded by the world and yet are carried on in flat contradiction to
> 5 the command of God, in accordance with all unrighteousness which is in the world. From all these things we shall be separated.[2]

Fifth, they only acknowledged their church pastors, whose role was to administer the sacraments, to teach and discipline the people, and, when necessary, impose the 'ban'. Sixth, they renounced violence and military service 'since only the magistrate can use the sword to punish the wicked and protect the good'. Finally, they refused to swear oaths to either civil or religious authorities arguing, 'We cannot fulfil that which we promise when we swear, for we cannot change the very least on us'.

Each of these beliefs was grounded in the Bible and, as each Anabaptist leader had his own opinion on how to interpret it, it is not surprising that there were several variations. Some sects rejected social conventions, abandoned their worldly possessions and lived a life of communal Christian simplicity. Others refused to pay church tithes, civic taxes or the interest on loans. A number were heavily influenced by mysticism and spiritualism. Several were millenarian and proclaimed that the world would end. Hut, for example, believed this would occur in 1528 and Augsburg would be the New Jerusalem; Hoffman thought it would end in 1533 and he went to Strasbourg to witness it; while Bockelson was convinced Münster would be the promised land in 1534. Though all radicals were willing to die for their beliefs, a small number were ready to use violence on the ungodly. Some practised familiarism (the belief that religion was a matter of love rather than faith) and others believed in Christology (Christ was born without Mary losing her virginity). Most lived in closed, isolated communities. Some, like the Moravian Hutterites, sought to perpetuate their sect by insisting on arranged marriages, while the Mennonites in Münster introduced polygamy. This practice, although exceptional, is confirmation that Anabaptism was a patriarchal faith: there were twice as many women as men in Münster and their leader, Bockelson, decreed that men could have as many wives as they wished and it was illegal for women to remain unmarried.

Given the wide variety of unconventional social, economic, political and religious practices, it is not surprising that these sects were described as 'Schwarmer' (fanatic) and all were persecuted in varying degrees. J. M. Stayer has suggested that at least 4,000 Anabaptists were burned, drowned or executed in the course of the sixteenth century.[3] That they were able to survive at all was due to their stoicism, the firm social control exercised by their communal leaders, and their ability to hide their faiths to avoid persecution.

b) Varieties of Radicalism

In the years immediately preceding the Peasants' Wars of 1524–26 (see page 40), radicalism was to be found in many areas of Germany, Switzerland and Moravia. In 1521 Andreas Karlstadt pushed for more church reforms in Wittenberg and, assisted by the arrival of the Zwickau prophets – three followers of Thomas Müntzer who had been expelled from the Saxon town – introduced further changes. The prophets foretold that the world would soon end, Germany would be invaded by the Turks, and all priests would be killed unless they got married. In 1521 monks were stoned, services interrupted, and vernacular communion celebrated in both kinds. As weavers, miners, peasants and students threatened the town with the unwholesome prospect of disorder masquerading as democracy, Luther returned from his refuge in Wartburg. By March 1522, order had been restored. Karlstadt retired, first to Thuringia and then to Zurich, before ending his turbulent life teaching at the university of Basle.

Müntzer had meanwhile been expelled from Zwickau before settling in Allstedt, Saxony, in 1523. He advocated adult baptism, the marriage of priests, the communal use of property, and claimed that anyone could be a priest because all authority was derived from the people. Furthermore, his belief in redemption through suffering encouraged many to welcome martyrdom. Indeed, he himself had declared, 'I desire nothing else but my own persecution, so that all may profit and be converted through me'.[4] Müntzer was a prolific preacher, writer and teacher. He saw himself as a crusader of truth and referred to Luther as Dr Liar, Father Pussyfoot, the Wittenberg pope. Peasant disturbances in 1524 gave him his chance to urge them to take up arms and overthrow those 'fantastic perverts, those knaves, the godless'. 'Let not your sword grow cold', he cried, 'let it not be blunted. Smite, cling, clang, on the anvil of Nimrod, and cast the tower to the ground.' Allstedt soon found his ideas too revolutionary and he again took to the road, reaching Mühlhausen, one of the centres of the peasants' revolt. Assuming the role of peasant leader, he was captured and executed in 1525.

The earliest Swiss Anabaptists in 1523 rejected Zwingli's ideas as being too conservative. They renounced infant baptism, swearing oaths, paying tithes and performing military service, and demanded that they be allowed to appoint their own pastors. Such unorthodox demands were but a short step away from rejecting all civil authority and establishing a separate, self-governing congregation. In 1525 a group known as the Swiss Brethren was formed in Zurich. Led by Simon Stumpf, Felix Mantz and Conrad Grebel, all well-educated men from comfortable backgrounds, the sect publically debated the question of child baptism with Zwingli. It was, perhaps, inevitable that they would lose but the manner with which they accepted their defeat left something to be desired. They turned against the magistrates and called upon the people to rise up and join the peasants' revolt in nearby Schaffhausen, Waldshut and St Gallen. Zurich magistrates acted quickly. Grebel and several of his followers were arrested and Mantz was drowned in the lake in 1527, the first Swiss Anabaptist martyr.

The threat of the peasants' wars led to a widespread persecution of Anabaptists in Switzerland and southern Germany. Many of the Swiss Brethren sought refuge in Basle until 1529, and then in Berne in the 1530s. Some went to Strasbourg, until they were forced to move and many left for Moravia, where they joined other persecuted groups from Hesse, Swabia, Thuringia and the Tyrol. Most German Anabaptists were influenced by Müntzer's mysticism; some, like Hans Hut, Melchior Rinck and Hans Denck, met up in the Rhineland in

1525. Hut died in prison in Augsburg in 1528 but his ideas remained popular in central and southern Germany, Austria and Moravia, and were continued by Jakob Hutter and his 200 followers, known as the Moravian Brethren. The Moravian nobility protected dissenters and perhaps as many as 20,000 Anabaptists had established refugee settlements by the 1530s, safe in the knowledge that they would not be persecuted.

Dutch Anabaptists had a dramatic impact on the development of continental radicalism. Melchior Hoffman, a Lutheran preacher from Livonia, experienced apocalyptic visions in the 1520s and, after steadily rejecting Luther's views on justification and the real presence, was expelled from several Baltic towns before finally settling in Strasbourg in 1529. There he called upon the people to opt out of the established church and join the 'gathered church', proclaiming that the world would end in 1533. When he was arrested that year for inciting rebellion, his ability to lead his people did effectively end. He died in prison ten years later. However, his ideas which were a mixture of spiritualism and millenarianism, became popular in the Netherlands in Emden and Amsterdam, where he had briefly preached in 1530, and some of his followers, known as Melchiorites, settled in Münster in north-west Germany (see case study below). Most Dutch Anabaptists were totally opposed to violence and had been appalled by the excesses perpetrated in Münster. Some, like David Joris, preached that the godless would soon be punished and that the Netherlands would witness the Second Coming; many followed Menno Simons, a priest from Friesland, who rejected some of the more extreme social practices of the Melchiorites yet retained radical theological beliefs such as Christology. Tolerant and peace-loving, the Mennonites were the least harmful of the radical groups and yet, labelled the 'enemies of truth' by Protestants and Catholics alike, they were persecuted wherever they went.

c) Case study: Münster

Münster was a small German town near to the Dutch border, protected by the Lutheran, Philip of Hesse, and governed by its annually elected council. The enforced resignation of the bishop of Münster in 1531 was accompanied by the arrival of Lutheran preachers and, in the course of the next two years, thousands of Dutch and German Anabaptists. Amid growing social and economic distress, and the sighting of comets which seemed to confirm that the Second Coming was imminent, a majority of radical Protestants won control of the council in February 1534. In this way, an Anabaptist government led by two Melchiorites, Jan Matthys of Haarlem and Jan Bockelson of Leyden, was established and a unique social revolution took place. Every citizen was ordered to be re-baptised in the market-place or face expulsion. Some 2,000 Catholics and Lutherans left but a far larger number of Anabaptists arrived. Ordinances enforced the communal sharing of goods, money and property, and polygamy became legal – Bockelson had 15 wives.

While Münster was undergoing internal reforms, its ousted bishop organised a counter-attack by hiring mercenaries who laid siege to it for the next 16 months. As tension rose in the enclosed community, order and resistance were maintained by passing penal laws for offences such as lying and quarrelling, as well as for more serious crimes like murder. Critics of the government were imprisoned or silenced, and death was often summary. When in June 1535 the town fell to a surprise attack from a combined Catholic and Lutheran army, more than 800 Anabaptists were executed. Among the dead was Bockelson, whose tongue was ripped out with red-hot pincers and whose body was left in a cage suspended from the church tower. Münster was returned to the Catholic bishop and order was slowly restored. This was the last Anabaptist attempt to reform world order through violence; thereafter, most radical sects practised a voluntary and peaceful withdrawal from society.

3 Calvin and Geneva

KEY ISSUES What were Calvin's main theological beliefs? How did they change the religious and social condition of Geneva?

PROFILE OF JOHN CALVIN

-Profile-

Born in 1509 in Noyon, France, the son of a lawyer, Calvin studied theology and law at university but the death of his father in 1531 and his return to Paris caused him to turn away from Catholicism. Convinced that he was 'chosen by God to proclaim the truth', his Protestant views were unwelcome in Paris and, between 1534 and 1536, he travelled to Switzerland, Germany and Italy, before arriving in Geneva in 1536. Having just published his *Institutes of the Christian Religion*, he was a well-known figure among French refugees and was persuaded to help reform the city. His strict sense of discipline, however, allied to his insistence that the council must submit to clerical control, proved unpalatable and he was expelled in 1538. For three years, he lived in Strasbourg, learned much from the theologian Bucer, and wrote several works before being tempted back to Geneva in 1541, where he remained until his death in 1564.

a) Calvin and his Theology

Calvin's main theological beliefs were first set out in six chapters in the *Institutes of the Christian Religion*, published in 1536. Thereafter, as he expanded and clarified his ideas, it was revised three times until the final edition of 1559 comprised four books and 80 chapters. Like all the other Protestant reformers, Calvin denounced indulgences, celibacy, pilgrimages, fasting and superstitious practices, and believed in only two sacraments, baptism and holy communion. Much of his thinking was conditioned by his scholastic and humanist education and by the ideas of Erasmus and the first generation of Protestant reformers. In fact, although he had much in common with Luther and Zwingli, his ideas were far closer to those of Bucer. He attached less significance to the Eucharist and, although he believed in the spiritual presence of Christ, he did not allow himself to be drawn into theological disputes over the meaning of consubstantiation, which had dogged the earlier reformers. Indeed, the doctrine of justification by faith was of greater significance to him. Those with faith, he contended, would be sure of salvation (a doctrine known as single predestination); those without faith would be damned (double predestination). However, why some were elected and others damned was a mystery to him and beyond human reason. According to the Scriptures, man could only be redeemed by the grace of God, and 'without regard to human worth'. Although both Luther and Zwingli had denied free will and, by implication, agreed with the doctrine of predestination, neither had developed the notion of double predestination, which made Calvinists certain of their own exclusive salvation.

Calvin did not have an original mind – the organisation of pastoral care, psalm singing and the establishment of an academy, for example, were all based on what he had seen in Strasbourg. But he had one distinctive quality which he brought to the Reformation: he could explain complex ideas clearly to a lay audience. Calvin had been trained as a lawyer and not as a priest or a monk. He was therefore able to bring a fresh approach to old ideas and to construct a logical, coherent and intelligible theology without the confusion and complexities that characterised the earliest Protestant doctrines. Above all, he created a church organisation that would embrace social and moral issues as well as religion, one which would protect the pure from the impure and the saved from the damned. In his sermons he preached fire and brimstone, covering subjects as diverse as greedy merchants and magisterial failings to immoral behaviour and scriptural ignorance. One Christmas Eve, for example, he declared: 'Can't you see the blasphemies and scandals and immorality everywhere? The whole world is debauched and every day I see that Geneva's impiety is so great that the city resembles, as it were, a stinking cesspool of hell'. Individuals in the congregation were pointed out and embarrassed; no one was spared.

b) Genevan Politics and Society

Calvin set out his reform programme in the *Ecclesiastical Ordinances* in 1541. Five years earlier, when he first arrived in Geneva, the city was in a state of turmoil. The 10,000 inhabitants were governed by four 'Syndics', who were elected by a General Council comprising the principal citizens. The traditional overlords, the duke of Savoy and the bishop of Geneva, had been expelled in 1527 but continued to threaten the city's autonomy in order to regain control. France also had claims to Genevan lands but a more serious threat came from neighbouring Berne, a member of the Swiss Confederation, which was keen to draw Geneva into its orbit. Political factions kept the city council divided: some councillors feared a loss of freedom if they became a Bernese client; others feared isolation if they did not, and this would play into the hands of Savoy and the bishop.

In the 1530s, political insecurity was accompanied by religious confusion. Berne, a Zwinglian canton, was hopeful of converting Geneva and instigated reforms such as closing monasteries, seizing church revenue and setting up a hospital for the poor. The arrival of Lutheran preachers and French Protestant refugees, however, produced more radical changes: the mass was suspended in 1535 and, in the following year, the council voted in favour of establishing a Protestant reformation. It was against this unstable background that Guillaume Farel, a native preacher, invited Calvin who was visiting Geneva to stay and restore some discipline to the city. A majority on the council at first favoured a mixture of Protestant reform and Catholic tradition, all controlled by the magistrates. When Calvin insisted that every citizen should accept his 'confession of faith' or leave the city, there was uproar and, amid a torrent of abuse, it was Calvin and Farel who departed.

For the next three years, the Articulant faction in the council drew the city closer to Berne, ceding territorial rights and privileges, as well as church revenue in return for political and military support. By 1540, the prevailing feeling among Genevans was that they had surrendered too much to the Bernese, and a rival faction, the Guillarmins, was swept to power in the local elections. Once again Calvin was invited to return to reform the Genevan church. He accepted, reluctantly, partly because he realised that as an employee of the city, he would have to compromise many of his proposals but also because he was one of four ministers responsible for the spiritual welfare of the citizens and he had a low regard for his fellow pastors. They were, he claimed, 'rude and self-conceited', and without ' zeal and learning', and, for the next four years, until they were removed from their posts, relations between the ministers were extremely acrimonious.

Calvin's *Ecclesiastical Ordinances* were the blue-print of his reformed church. Lay and clerical officers governed the 'visible church'. It was divided into four orders of pastors (alternatively referred to as 'ministers'), doctors, deacons and elders, who were elected annually by the Small Council of 25 male citizens, which in turn was elected by the General Council of 200. Each order had a clearly defined function. The pastors were 'to proclaim the Word of God, to teach, and to administer the sacraments, admonish, exhort and reprove publically and privately'. People were expected to attend church every Sunday and it was possible to hear a sermon every day and at different times of the day so that no one had any excuse not to be present. All pastors belonged to the Venerable Company and were required to meet once a week for Bible discussions. The doctors were responsible for education and were 'to instruct the faithful in sound doctrine so that the purity of the Gospel is not corrupted by ignorance or evil opinions'. They were assisted by a catechism, written by Calvin in 1542, that was divided into five parts: faith, the law, prayer, the Word of God, and the sacraments. The deacons were responsible for running the city's hospital and the welfare of the poor. They were 'to receive, distribute and protect the goods of the poor' and 'to take care of the sick and administer the pittance for the poor'. Finally, the elders were to uphold levels of public morality, 'to watch over the lives of everyone, to admonish amiably those they see in error and leading disorderly lives'.

Those who publicly broke the codes of conduct expected of Calvinists were called to account before the Consistory. This was an ecclesiastical court which comprised 12 lay elders and all of the pastors. In 1542 there were only nine pastors but the number steadily increased until, in 1555, they were in a majority and, by 1564, there were 19. Calvin had always intended putting them in charge of both lay and clerical discipline but he had to wait 14 years before this was achieved. Even then, every punishment had to be sanctioned by the city's magistrates although, in practice, the division between the civil and spiritual courts was far from clear-cut. Meeting most Thursdays for between three and four hours, the Consistory had the authority to investigate and reprimand anyone. Inappropriate behaviour, such as sexual promiscuity, dancing, singing outside church, excessive drinking, gambling and wearing ostentatious clothes, were all heavily censured. Many laws concerning people's moral behaviour had in fact been introduced in the 1530s; Calvin simply reinforced them and added some of his own. Ecclesiastical discipline would therefore promote social discipline. And the court did more than act as a tribunal; it was used to discover whether people could recite the Lord's Prayer, the Ten Commandments and the Apostles' Creed, and if they could not, then they were ordered to return when they could. The court was also used as a means of resolving private quarrels and arbitrating in disputes, in much the same way as the bishop's court had once done.

At first most cases brought before the court concerned religious deviation – missing sermons, making mistakes when reciting the catechism in French and believing in Catholic superstitious practices – but by 1550, this category totalled just 14 per cent of all cases. In fact, personal and public disputes accounted for more than 50 per cent and sexual misconduct for more than one-third of all investigations. This suggests that the city had become more Protestant in the first decade since Calvin's return and that the Consistory was more effective in imposing religious uniformity. Punishments ranged from gentle rebukes to public confession, from exclusion from communion to excommunication, and, on rare occasions, exile or death. Let us take swearing in public as an illustration. Anyone who swore a 'frivolous oath' was made to kneel down and kiss the ground and if they swore 'blasphemously' they had to spend a day and a night in prison on bread and water, and then obtain a pardon from a pastor. If anyone spoke 'spitefully' of God, he was 'put in the stocks for three hours and, from there, being led to prison and fed on bread and water until the following Sunday when he shall be led to the door of the church where he shall ask for God's pardon while holding a lighted candle. Those guilty of a second offence will be beaten and banished from the city'.[5]

The power of the Consistory depended on its ability to impose excommunication and to use this weapon in moderation. In general, those brought before the court received three warnings before excommunication was passed and, although such sentences were fairly common in this period, averaging five a week, bans were usually lifted quite quickly. Several cases, however, assumed a much higher profile than Calvin would have wished and these have been seen by his critics and by hostile historians alike as illustrative of his narrow-minded intolerance. Sebastian Castellio, for example, a school teacher, was expelled from Geneva in 1544 for claiming that the biblical 'Song of Songs' was an erotic poem. In 1546 Pierre Ameaux publicly accused Calvin of corrupting Geneva with 'false doctrine', of refusing to teach Latin and seeking to rule the city. Although Ameaux was a respected councillor, he was ordered to walk to the centre of the city, dressed only in a shirt and carrying a torch, and there beg forgiveness for his errors from the magistrates, Calvin and God. Jacques Gruet was executed in 1547 for ridiculing the Christian faith by allegedly trying to 'reduce to nothing the teaching of Moses'. He had also somewhat unwisely alleged that Calvin was a French agent. Jerome Bolsec in 1551 voiced criticisms of Calvin's theology of predestination and was first imprisoned and then exiled. But by far the most notorious victim was Michael Servetus, a Spanish born humanist, who questioned the doctrine of the Trinity, denounced infant baptism and rejected *sola fide*. Servetus's book, *The Restoration of Christianity* (1553), was universally condemned and Calvin declared that, if Servetus ever visited Geneva, he would 'never let him get away alive'. In 1553 he was arrested in France but escaped and made his way to Geneva in disguise. However, when he was discovered, he was charged with heresy and burned at the stake.

In each of these cases and in his subsequent correspondence, Calvin tried to appear as the defender of Christian values and a man of moderation. His enemies on the council, led by the Perrinist faction, seized their chance to portray him as an interfering, unforgiving and arrogant foreigner. At the heart of this faction was Ami Perrin, a member of the Small Council and captain-general of the city's militia. His company had been censored by the Consistory for wearing an ostentatious uniform and being unruly, and Ami and his supporters were determined to bring Calvin down. Moreover, Ami's wife, Francesca, had been brought before the court on a charge of dancing in public. Both she and Ami enjoyed dancing and resented being told what they could and could not do. More generally, the Perrinists and many Genevans disliked the way their city was being run by Frenchmen – only one pastor was a native Genevan – and more than 7,000 refugees had entered the city in the early 1550s. Matters came to a head in May 1555. A financial crisis in the city had made the presence of wealthy French aristocrats and merchants very desirable and many had gained citizen status and could vote in the council elections. When the Perrinists voiced their objections, they were narrowly defeated and then voted off the council. A minority of them panicked and began a riot which resulted in the leading members of the faction being exiled or condemned to death. Ami and his wife were among those who fled the city. To the majority of Genevans, Calvin seemed indispensable and his reformation was at last secure.

Modern historians now appreciate the contrast between the years of insecurity, 1541–1555, when Calvin's ideas were consistently compromised and his authority challenged, and the last ten years of his life when his position was secure. In 1547 he was twice brought before the Consistory and cautioned for remarks made in his sermons; in 1548 and 1552, he was again reprimanded for calling the magistrates 'gargoyle monkeys' that 'vomit forth their blasphemies as supreme decrees'; and in 1552 he had to defend himself before the Small Council for refusing to baptise a child with the name of Claude because it was a popular saint's name which he considered unchristian. While Calvin and the ministers nearly always prevailed, they faced constant opposition until 1555. Thereafter, Calvin ruled supreme. As more refugees became citizens and were elected to the councils, so he extended the Reformation. Ministers assumed control of the Consistory when they were allowed to veto the selection of elders, and even the Syndics, who ruled the city, acknowledged the nascent ministerial authority by ceasing to bring their baton – a symbol of secular power – to meetings of the Consistory. In the *Ecclesiastical Ordinances* he had stated his intention to 'found a college for the instruction of those young people who are to be prepared for the ministry and for civil government', but Genevan politics and financial limitations had prevented its opening for 18 years. In 1559 he opened an academy for the training of future leaders and missionaries (today it is a university) and, at his death in 1564, it had 1,500 students. In his view, education had a crucial role to play: it imparted discipline and spiritual guidance, and the detailed curriculum, school regulations and careful selection of professors, reflected Calvin's wish to 'indoctrinate' as well as to 'instruct' the young. Geneva thus became the model of the reformed Protestant Church and its academy the mainspring of an international movement.

4 Conclusion

Lutheranism was not the only evangelical faith in the 1520s. Zwinglianism in Switzerland and south Germany and a range of radical sects in Germany, Switzerland, the Netherlands and Moravia, demonstrate the variety of competing reform movements. Each had its own unique attractions and each carried serious limitations. The military defeat of Zurich and Zwingli's death in 1531 deprived the faith of its charismatic leader, and the Swiss Confederation of its backbone. The Anabaptists, on the other hand, never had more than a minority following due to their revolutionary beliefs and their desire to divorce themselves from mainstream society. And, as we have seen in Chapter 3, Lutheranism was essentially a German movement, somewhat equivocal in its doctrine and far less radical than either Zwinglianism or Anabaptism. The way was open for Calvinism to become the leading Protestant faith in the second half of the sixteenth century. In the 1550s, more than 30 printing houses in Geneva produced anti-Catholic propaganda, as well as Calvinist evangelical and theological tracts, ready for export. The clear, logical exposition of the *Institutes* and Calvin's accessible prose style, whether in Latin or French, appealed to literate urban groups in most European countries (see Chapter 7). As a second generation reformer *par excellence*, Calvin had established in Geneva a church that was reformed and a society that was transformed beyond all recognition. But how would Calvinism fare in the future without the inspiring leadership of its founder? Would Geneva go the same way as Zurich, and recede into the backwater of European Protestantism?

Footnotes
1. U. Zwingli, *Sämtlich Werke*, vol. 1, p. 459.
2. www.cc.ukans.edu/~hisite/gilbert/15.
3. J.M. Stayer, 'The Anabaptists and the sects', in *New Cambridge Modern History* (CUP, 1999), vol. iv, p.143.

4. P. Matheson (trans. and ed.), *Collected Works of Thomas Müntzer* (T and T. Clark, Edinburgh, 1988), p. 35.
5. G.R. Potter and M. Greengrass (eds.), *John Calvin* (Arnold, 1983), p. 80.

Summary diagram
'Zwinglianism, Radicalism and Calvinism'

Similarities in the beliefs of Zwinglianism, Anabaptism and Calvinism

2 sacraments (baptism and communion), predestination, clerical marriage, removal of church images, no fasting during Lent, *sola scriptura*, vernacular services.

Differences in the beliefs of Zwinglianism, Anabaptism and Calvinism

	Zwinglianism	Anabaptism	Calvinism
Baptism:	infant baptism	adult baptism	infant baptism
Bible:	emphasis on the New Testament	emphasis on the Old Testament	emphasis on the entire Bible
Eucharist:	sacraments were representative	revelation by the Holy Spirit	Christ was spiritually present
Salvation:	predestination known only by God	predestination by an act of Jesus	double predestination known only by God
Church music:	none	none	congregational singing of psalms
Church-state relations:	Church should be subject to the state	Church should be separate from the state	discipline should be controlled by the state

Answering structured and essay questions on Chapter 4

You will rarely be given an opportunity to answer a structured or essay question on Zwinglianism and radicalism except by way of a comparison with Luther or Calvin. Geneva and Calvinism, on the other hand, is a much more popular topic and the following questions are typical of what can be asked:

1. Compare Zwingli and Calvin as religious reformers.
2. 'Geneva was the power house of the Calvinist Reformation.' Discuss.
3. How far did Calvin create a new society as well as a new Church in Geneva?

Let us examine Question 3. 'How far' is an evaluative question and extremely common at A Level. Logically, you can say that Calvin created a completely new society and Church, that he introduced changes in both society and religion which were not totally new or that he brought in no changes at all. While it is always worth considering the 'extreme' positions, most often history is rarely black-and-white and you will probably go for some sort of middle position. It does not matter what words you choose as long as their meaning is clear and they fit your interpretation of events. Once you have decided on how to interpret this question and you are satisfied that you have acquired enough evidence to support your argument, put your ideas on paper in an essay plan. This can be done point by point or diagrammatically. You will need to think critically at this stage to ensure that your approach is relevant and coherent. It may help if you number your points in order of importance; this will enable you to begin with the most significant idea and to work logically through your list when you write your essay.

Start by defining the terms of the question. In this question, the key words are 'create' and 'new'; next, break the topic down into smaller sub-divisions, on each of which you would subsequently write a whole paragraph; and, finally, outline your argument. In Question 3, this means deciding what was 'new' about social, educational, moral and religious affairs in Geneva. This will probably involve comparing Geneva in 1541 and 1564 (when Calvin died) or, alternatively, with other reformed churches, such as Lutheranism, Zwinglianism and Anabaptism. In fact, the arguments/comparisons that could be given are endless. All that is important is that you do have a relevant argument and that you can support it with evidence. At the end of the essay, in the concluding paragraph, return once again to the central issue – 'how far' – and hammer home your view.

5 The English Reformation

POINTS TO CONSIDER

The simplest questions in History frequently produce the most complex answers. This is particularly so when we ask: what was the English Reformation? When and why did it begin, and how was it accomplished? Most historians agree that at some time in the half century after 1529 England became a Protestant country, but there is continuing disagreement as to the nature, extent and manner by which it was achieved. This chapter endeavours to explore some of these themes, focusing on the main developments between 1529 and 1571.

KEY DATES

1529 Wolsey fell from office; parliament convened to help Henry get a divorce.
1532 English clergy submitted to the king.
1533 Cranmer became archbishop of Canterbury; Act in Restraint of Appeals.
1534 Act of Supremacy.
1536 Act of Ten Articles; smaller monasteries dissolved.
1539 Act of Six Articles; English Bible published.
1549 Cranmer produced an English Prayer Book.
1552 Second Edwardian Prayer Book published.
1554 Pole became archbishop of Canterbury; Anglo-papal relations restored.
1555 Burning of Protestants began.
1559 Elizabethan Church Settlement established.
1563 Convocation issued 38 Articles.
1570 Excommunication of Elizabeth.
1571 Act of 39 Articles.

1 Henry VIII and the English Church

KEY ISSUES What was the condition of the Church in England in 1529? Why did England and Rome separate in 1534? What were the main changes and responses by 1547?

a) The Condition of the Church in England in 1529

In Chapter 2 we pointed out that the Catholic Church in England was in a sound condition in the early sixteenth century. The majority of clergy worked hard for little remuneration and fulfilled their pastoral duties to the best of their ability. Bishops like Fisher (of Rochester), Longland (Lincoln) and West (Ely), who reformed their diocesan administration and improved the quality of their clergy, were excellent examples of dedication and honesty. Even Wolsey, a much maligned figure, regularly visited Bath and Wells during his tenure as bishop (1518-23), supervised national visitations and drafted plans to reorganise English and Irish bishoprics in 1529. While it remains true that the education of many parish priests was poor, with few having university degrees, there was no apparent shortage of ordinands entering the Church. Indeed, the 1520s saw the peak of more than half a century of expansion in the diocese of Lincoln, and this was not exceptional. There were complaints and criticisms from a minority of merchants, lawyers and humanist-trained clergymen, who claimed that the Church was corrupt and in need of reform, and no one gained any pleasure from paying taxes to Rome or being publicly admonished in the church courts. Allegations of sexual misconduct, lax behaviour and financial irregularities were made against the regular clergy but the surviving evidence suggests that few complaints were substantiated. In the diocese of Lincoln, only a handful of 111 monastic houses were identified as corrupt and, in the north and west of England, gifts to monasteries and nunneries continued well into the early 1530s. The Carthusian, Bridgettine and Observant Franciscans received regular endowments and long established monastic houses such as Glastonbury and Syon were still attracting large numbers of novices.

Was the Church in urgent need of reform in 1529? There is little evidence to suggest this. Most historians now discount the substance behind the anti-clerical literature that poured from the press in the late 1520s and 1530s. Certainly the attack on the wealth and privileges of the clergy by the Lutheran Simon Fish in *The Supplication for the Beggars* (1529) went down well in London but this does not mean that his jibes were shared elsewhere. Indeed, the complaints of high and arbitrary probate and funeral fees, which were voiced by some MPs in the 1529 session of parliament, need to be seen in context. Several MPs were lawyers who resented the loss of business to the church courts and both probate and mortuary complaints were of recent origin, a result of a plague epidemic in 1528. It also seems clear that church courts did not cause serious problems; in fact, only a handful of tithe cases were dealt with each year and London, which has been traditionally regarded as a centre of anti-clericalism, was probably untypical.

Most people appear to have been very much attached to traditional clerical practices. Much of their life was conditioned by the church calendar: more than 50 saints' days, 40 feast days and the 40 days of Lent were honoured each year, and their involvement in parish ceremonies, such as Candlemas and Ash Wednesday, was a demonstration of local unity. Believing in saints (local, biblical and patron), venerating images, collecting relics, going on pilgrimages, joining guilds, founding chantries and buying indulgences were all common features of English parochial life in the 1520s. Churchwardens' accounts and wills attest to the popular devotion throughout the country. Lights, candles and lamps burned in every parish church in memory of the dead, while the living continued to establish chantries well into the 1530s. Endowments were given and most parish churches were well equipped with ornaments, mass-books, copes and vestments. Historians have often doubted the degree to which people understood their religious beliefs but it seems evident that the literate gained their understanding from Latin primers, catechisms and devotional books, while everyone could see the images on altar-pieces, rood screens and wall paintings, and they could hear itinerant preachers and watch travelling players. Most people accepted what they saw and heard even if they could not explain their beliefs. By their own standards, they were devout and religious people.

The impact of Erasmus in England was confined to an academic élite and a small court circle. Although his ideas remained popular in Cambridge and may have accounted for the interest there in biblical humanism and church reform, few scholars and clerics showed much interest in Erasmianism. Thomas More remained a good friend but found his humanist tendencies curbed by his loyalty to the state and devotion to the orthodox faith. Wolsey had seemed perfectly placed to apply the 'new learning' to the Church but his first duty was to serve the king and, while Henry liked to be portrayed as a Renaissance prince, in reality he had little genuine interest in academia and even less in church reform. Once he had publicly condemned Luther's rejection of the seven sacraments in 1521 and earned the gratitude of the papacy with the title 'Defender of the Faith', the king was convinced that Luther was a heretic and should be condemned.

Lutheran ideas entered England in 1520. Books were burned in Cambridge and London, and archbishop Warham informed Wolsey that he had learned that several students at Oxford were 'infected with the heresies of Luther and others of that sort'. A small number of clerics and merchants took up Lutheranism; many were Cambridge graduates like Barnes, Bilney, Coverdale, Latimer and Tyndale. And in spite of royal proclamations, heretical books continued to be printed and circulated in London and Cambridge. Wolsey encouraged the bishops to persecute Lutherans, and Tunstall, bishop of London, personally targeted Tyndale. In 1525 Tyndale fled to Wittenberg, published the New Testament in English and adapted Lutheran ideas in a series of commentaries. Tyndale was the first Englishman to introduce continental reforms to England. In many respects, his views reflected a Lollard tradition and historians have noted that Lutheranism was most firmly established in areas where Lollardy had once existed (see page 13). Although it remains true that at first the Church found it hard to distinguish between Lollards and Lutherans, there were in fact clear differences: the former questioned the real presence of Christ, detested the worshipping of images and shrines and, under Tyndale's scholarship, developed a moral legalism; the latter believed in the real presence, tolerated the veneration of images, and believed that all subjects had a duty to obey their ruler.

Henry did not like Tyndale's English Bible – there had been a Lollard Bible in circulation for years and he did not like that either – but he was interested in another of Tyndale's works, the *Obedience of a Christian Man*, published in 1528. It was Anne Boleyn, Henry's mistress, who handed the king a copy. In his book, Tyndale rejected papal claims to temporal and spiritual headship and developed a theory in which all subjects had a duty to obey the ruler and the law but the ruler also had an obligation to govern in their best interest. We can only surmise whether Anne was motivated by her desire to help Henry get a divorce and so clear the way for her to become queen or whether her hatred for Wolsey, who did not favour a divorce, was fired by her Protestant leanings and a desire to see the king reform the English Church. She certainly advocated church reform, promoted preachers like Shaxton and Latimer, and had contacts with reformist groups at the French court. Henry, like most Englishmen, was unwilling to accept Luther's theological reasoning on the Eucharist, but the German's successful denial of papal authority and the subsequent political autonomy exercised by Lutheran princes will not have escaped his notice. In 1527 Henry had begun divorce proceedings against Katherine of Aragon. She had once been married to Henry's elder brother and, following his death, the papacy had permitted the king to marry her. Since then, she had failed to produce a son. In Henry's opinion, the papal consent had either been inadequate or unlawful; either way, God was punishing him for sleeping with Katherine and the time had come to dispense with her. When pope Clement VII refused Henry's request, the fate of the English Church lay in the balance.

b) The Break from Rome

In October 1529, Henry dismissed his lord chancellor, Thomas Wolsey. This most powerful of men had paid the price for failing to get the king what he most desired – a divorce. That Henry was an orthodox Catholic and loyal servant of the pope is apparent from his concern that the divorce should be granted by God's representative on earth; and there is no indication that the king had a reformation of the Church in mind. In the course of the next five years, Henry would get a divorce, separate from Rome and be in a position to introduce reforms to the Church if he so wished. How did this situation arise? Historians, of course, have the benefit of hindsight and, in tracing back events from November 1534 (when Henry became Supreme

Head of the Church of England) to November 1529 (when parliament was convened), it is tempting to claim that the king and his parliament worked from the outset to achieve these ends. In fact, Henry's only real concern was to get a divorce, marry Anne Boleyn and produce a male heir. Some of his leading advisers, however, had additional objectives. Thomas Cromwell, for instance, who entered the king's council in 1531 and became royal secretary, had firm views on parliamentary sovereignty. He believed that the king in parliament had no superior. Together they could pressurise the pope into granting a divorce and, if necessary, procure it for the king without papal consent. Many common lawyers agreed with Christopher St German, who wrote in 1530 that 'jurisdiction over all temporal things belongs to the secular state'. Henry may well have concurred since 15 years earlier he had declared that 'Kings of England have never had any superior but God alone'.

Cromwell was not only a lawyer, MP and royal councillor, he was also a Protestant – though whether or not he can be called a Lutheran has been much debated. Certainly, he patronised English Lutherans like Tyndale and Barnes, and agreed with many of Luther's ideas but, given Henry's implacable stance against heresy, it seems unlikely that Cromwell held strong doctrinal views, at least not publicly. A second important adviser to the king was Thomas Cranmer. As a Cambridge academic, he assisted Henry in 1530 in canvassing continental universities to support the king's request for a divorce and, together with Edward Foxe, bishop of Hereford, presented substantial evidence to convince the king that he had the authority (or 'imperium') to summon bishops and procure a divorce independently of the pope. Significantly, Cranmer was part of the Boleyn faction and was duly rewarded when the king made him archbishop of Canterbury in 1533. The leading nobles in Henry's council, especially the dukes of Norfolk and Suffolk, were more critical of bishops than of popes but, as straws in the wind, waited to see what the king intended to do, and then followed him. And this was the problem. Henry simply did not know how to proceed. When he turned to Cromwell, Cranmer and Anne, they urged him to grasp the papal nettle; but if he listened to more orthodox bishops like Warham, Fisher and Tunstall or turned to More, the lord chancellor, he was reminded that relations with the pope must not be compromised. Parliament also failed to give a lead. Though in regular attendance since 1529, it achieved little before 1531 and was split three ways: some MPs favoured divorce, some opposed and some, perhaps the majority, sat on the fence.

The historian Geoffrey Elton has demonstrated the vital part that Cromwell played from 1532 in drafting parliamentary bills, securing their approval and silencing opposition both within and outside parliament. How far Cromwell was the architect or executor of the legislation remains debatable but it seems likely that he had the conviction which the king lacked to see through mutually held ideas. So far the

English clergy had staved off parliamentary attacks on canon law, accusations of *praemunire* (owing allegiance to the pope rather than to the king) and had accepted that Henry was head of the Church in England 'as far as the law of Christ allows'. In spite of these anti-clerical attacks, the pope showed no sign of granting the king a divorce. From May 1532, effective pressure was exerted on the English clergy and they submitted to the king without reservation. Thomas More significantly resigned. He could not continue to serve the king and satisfy his conscience. Parliament then attacked the pope's chief source of revenue – annates – threatening to withhold them if he did not cooperate; further, if he refused to consecrate English bishops, it was declared that Henry had the authority. This was the first challenge to the pope's spiritual jurisdiction and, although the bill of annates was only to take effect after one year to give the pope sufficient time to respond, the bill became an act in 1533.

It was followed by the Act in Restraint of Appeals in April 1533. The preamble read: 'This realm of England is an Empire ... governed by one Supreme Head and King.' It was a defining moment in the whole affair because it denied the pope all jurisdiction in England and prevented English subjects from seeking help from Rome. Already in train were preparations for Cranmer, the newly appointed archbishop, to hear the divorce case and prevent Katherine from appealing against the judgement. Anne Boleyn played her part too – in January she became pregnant. There could be no delay in finalising a settlement. A divorce was granted in May, Henry and Anne were married in June, and a baby girl, Elizabeth, was born in September. By the end of 1533, the break from Rome was in all but name complete. In the following year, further legislation transferred all spiritual and temporal power from the pope to the king: he could elect bishops and abbots; he controlled the church courts; he was entitled to collect all clerical taxes; and, in November 1534, the Act of Supremacy confirmed that Henry was 'Supreme Head of the Church of England'.

c) The Henrician Reformation, 1535–47

In 1534 Cromwell was appointed vicegerent by Henry. Although the king determined doctrinal reforms in consultation with his bishops, this title gave Cromwell effective control of the Church. In these years until his death in 1540, he was the power behind the throne. It was Cromwell who sponsored William Marshall to produce an English Primer which described traditional forms of piety as 'superstitious' and 'full of lies and vanities', and who in 1535 translated a tract by Bucer that denounced the worship of images. It was also Cromwell who ordered a survey of all church property in 1535 and masterminded the dissolution of the monasteries. Church property had been seized and monks expelled on the continent in the 1520s but the English dissolution owed little to their experience. Initially some

372 houses worth less than £200 a year and with fewer than 12 inmates were closed down. The larger monasteries were exempt because they were 'right well kept and observed' but by 1540 these, too, had been dissolved. In all more than 800 religious houses were closed, over 11,000 monks, nuns and friars were dispossessed and a fundamental act of reform completed with minimal opposition. Although the pilgrimage of grace in 1536 demonstrated principally against the closure of smaller monasteries in the north of England, the 30,000 rebels also petitioned to restore the papal headship, re-establish holy days and rid England of Protestant heresy. Attachment to devotional institutions and their clergy was far greater in the north than in the south of England and they were right to suspect an evangelical hand at work. They blamed Cromwell, Audley (lord chancellor) and Rich (chancellor of the court of Augmentations) as 'mayntenters of the false sect of those heretiques and the first inventors and bryngands in of them'. But the closure owed as much to financial necessity as it did to doctrinal reform. The monasteries were wealthy institutions, worth some £163,000 *per annum* in rents alone and the crown urgently needed money. Indeed, many of the gentry, both Catholic and Protestant, subsequently shared in the spoils and, in acquiring so much church property, ensured that this reforming measure would not be reversed. Nevertheless, advocates of the dissolution, such as Hugh Latimer, sensed that the time was right to attack the concept of purgatory and implement a thorough-going Protestant Reformation.

In 1536 Cromwell sent letters to JPs, sheriffs and nobles to compel conservative-minded bishops to adopt a more reformed stance and he licensed itinerant preachers like Barnes, Garrett, Shaxton and Latimer, to spread reform. Publicists such as Richard Morrison and John Bale were employed to write anti-papal pamphlets and, in the case of Bale, to sponsor actors to perform biblical scenes which portrayed reformist ideas. At the same time, Cranmer urged the bishops to begin discouraging traditional beliefs in saints' days, pilgrimages, worshipping shrines and similar 'superstitious' practices, but not to question the doctrine of purgatory. Henry was well aware of the factionalism in his court, council and convocations, and was principally concerned with preserving unity and eradicating extremists. He may have personally softened his attitude towards Luther but he had no tolerance for sacramentarians and papalists. In 1535, seven monks and a priest were executed for denying the royal supremacy and 12 London Anabaptists were burned for heresy.

In July 1536 the first official statement of faith was pronounced by convocation: the Act of Ten Articles. This doctrine was based on the Wittenberg Articles, a statement drawn up by bishops Foxe and Heath, who had travelled to Saxony to see if Lutheran ideas could be implemented in England to the satisfaction of the king and reformers. The objective was 'unity and agreement'; the result was a compromise. Baptism, penance and the Eucharist were the only sacraments to be affirmed and justification by faith was endorsed, but the articles were orthodox on good works, masses for the dead, and the veneration of images and saints. Though the formulary was a compromise, it was undoubtedly a step towards establishing an evangelical church along continental lines. Royal injunctions in August introduced further changes: more than 100 holy days were to be cancelled from the liturgical calendar, and an English catechism on the Creed, Lord's Prayer and Ten Commandments was to be acquired by every parish church. Finally, all churches were ordered to purchase an English Bible. Based on Tyndale's edition of the New Testament and revised by Coverdale, some 9,000 Bibles were available for distribution in 1539. Cromwell supervised its publication and, to many, this would be his lasting monument to the English Reformation.

In spite of resistance from conservative bishops like Gardiner, Tunstall and Stokesley, who presented their views in the *Bishops' Book* (1537), new injunctions were issued in the following year. Works of faith, mercy and charity were all praised but shrines, places of pilgrimage, holy relics and the worshipping of religious images were condemned. As a result, the graves and memorabilia associated with saints, such as Thomas at Canterbury, Swithin at Winchester and Cuthbert at Durham, were classed as popish and superstitious, and thus redundant. The custom of burning candles, tapers and wax lights in front of images and pictures was also to cease, though the extent to which these reforms were enforced clearly varied from place to place. Bishop Lee of York, for example, ignored anything that he disagreed with, while Shaxton of Salisbury objected to all 'old foolish customs' and implemented the reforms. In general, there was more continuity than change. Six months later, Cromwell was receiving reports that the pope's name still appeared in the Matins' Book at Newbury, that images of Becket remained in the church windows at Henley-on-Thames, that the shrine of St Hugh remained in Lincoln cathedral and that the vicar of Enfield refused to buy an English Bible.

The winter of 1538/9 saw acts of iconoclasm and vandalism occur throughout the country. Such disturbances threatened public order and Catholic councillors convinced Henry that unless he put a stop to this unbridled reformation, anarchy would result. The king responded and in June 1539 gave his assent to the Act of Six Articles, a formulary which re-affirmed the seven sacraments and made no concessions to Protestantism. Cranmer, Goodrich, Barlow, Latimer and Shaxton argued against it in convocation but Henry and the conservatives prevailed. More than 200 arrests occurred in the next year and, although most were released, the tempo was set for the rest of the reign. It was apparent that the king had applied a brake to church reform; and those associated with evangelicalism now had to tread warily. Cranmer always retained the king's affection and protection, and realised the futility of pressing ahead with further changes. Cromwell, in contrast, was less cautious and fell victim of conservative opponents and the king's anger. Accused of heresy and treason, Cromwell was executed in June 1540. Two days later, the king ordered the burning of three English Lutherans and the execution of three papists, as if to underline his complete mastery. Luther was prompted to declare: 'Harry is pope, and the pope is Harry in England.'

After Cromwell's fall, a conservative reaction set in. Not only had the first reformation ended, it seemed as if many of the changes would be reversed. Certainly bishops Gardiner, Stokesley and Lee, and the Catholic duke of Norfolk, whose niece Katherine Howard became Henry's fifth wife in 1540, hoped to steer the doctrinally wavering king towards maintaining the orthodox faith. But the king was an unpredictable man. His mood swings were as variable as ever and his temper just as violent. Fluctuating between fear and assurance, Henry was shaken to discover his wife's adultery in 1542. This revelation and Katherine's subsequent execution did the Howard family untold harm and raised the hopes of the Protestant faction centred on Cranmer and Edward Seymour, uncle to Henry's only son. Such hopes, however, were quickly dispelled when Henry announced that all Protestant books except the Bible would be prohibited. Even this would soon be restricted to clerics, gentry and nobility since women and working men were considered incapable of reading it without committing blasphemy.

Henry's decision to marry a plain 31 year-old widow, Katherine Parr, who was known to have reformist inclinations, caught most people by surprise, but the king was looking for a companion not a confessor. In the meantime, Gardiner endeavoured to undermine Henry's trust in Cranmer. In general continental ideas held little attraction for English reformers but Cranmer was fully aware of the works of Zwingli, Melanchthon, Bucer and Luther. Indeed he had secretly married the niece of Osiander, the Lutheran preacher in Nuremberg. Gardiner was convinced that the archbishop was really a convert, and he may have been right. In 1544 Cranmer published a Litany in English, and in 1545 a Primer for schools that contained no saints' or feast days. Later that year he supported the dissolution of some 80 chantries which some preachers believed foreshadowed a rejection of purgatory. Even more worrying for Gardiner was the fact that the education of prince Edward had been entrusted to Katherine and evangelical tutors from Cambridge. Yet while Henry tolerated Cranmer's swing towards reform, he remained true to the traditional faith. When he died in January 1547, he did so as a Catholic, believing in purgatory and ordering masses for his soul. He left behind an English Church that was officially Catholic but in the hands of a small group of men and a boy-king who were determined to make it Protestant.

2 The Edwardian Reformation, 1547–53

> **KEY ISSUES** What were the main influences affecting religious change? How far was England a Protestant country by 1553?

a) Factors that Shaped the Edwardian Reformation

Edward was nine when his father died and, for the rest of his short life, he was guided and advised by a council of regency. In the most recent study of his reign, Dr MacCulloch has revealed the king's strong piety, his dislike of Catholicism and the support he gave to a minority of evangelical reformers.[1] Foremost among these was Cranmer. In 1547 his secretary, Ralph Morrice, commented: 'Now your grace may go forward in these matters, the opportunity of the time much better serving thereunto than in king Henry's days.' In fact Cranmer acted with moderation at first but steadily and resolutely transformed England into the leading Protestant country by 1553. He gave the Edwardian Reformation unity and direction and was responsible for its main developments. Assisting him were like-minded theologians such as Nicholas Ridley, bishop of London, and Robert Holgate of York, as well as more radically inclined bishops like Latimer of Worcester and Hooper of Gloucester.

A distinctive feature of the Edwardian Reformation was the influence of foreign Protestant emigrés such as Peter Martyr, Bernardino Ochino, Martin Bucer and John à Lasco. There had been contact between English and European reformers since 1536 and the years following the Act of Six Articles (1539) saw a steady stream of Protestants leave for the continent. Hooper, for example, had travelled to Strasbourg and Zurich. However, Charles V's victory over the German Lutheran army at Mühlberg (1547) led to an exodus of continental students and theologians. Bucer was appointed to Cambridge (1549–51) and Martyr to Oxford (1548–53) as lecturers in theology. Both men held Zwinglian views on the Eucharist and endeavoured to convert their students accordingly. The influence of both Zwinglian and Lutheran ideas may also be seen in several of Cranmer's works after 1548. Indeed, a steady correspondence was maintained between Bullinger in Zurich and Cranmer, Hooper and the Swiss reformers in England. Meanwhile, Ochino arrived from Strasbourg and preached in London and Canterbury. In 1548 he became the first superintendent of a 'stranger' church in London – a role later continued by à Lasco – and an indication that the capital was prepared to welcome Protestant refugees. Indeed Hooper hoped to see England assume the lead in European reform and clashed with Ridley as to how far London churches should be made available for these 'strangers'. During these years some 400 Flemings, 400 Germans and 5,000 French and Dutch settled in England, and all but Anabaptists were tolerated. Significantly the only heretics put to death in Edward's reign were two Unitarians, Joan Bocher and George van Parris in 1550.

The Tudor Reformation was shaped first and foremost by political affairs. In 1547 at Edward's accession, power in the council rested with his uncle Edward Seymour, the duke of Somerset, John Dudley, the earl of Warwick, and a handful of courtiers such as William Parr and William Paget, each of whom held evangelical views. Somerset was a cautious politician, more concerned about defeating Scotland in battle than leading a reformation in England, and allowed Cranmer a comparatively free hand in religious matters. Warwick assumed political control in 1549 and favoured a more rapid and progressive reform programme, which suited Cranmer. Nevertheless, as Cranmer charted a course towards a more Zwinglian church, the pace was never fast enough for men like Hooper, Latimer and Coverdale. There was little opposition to these changes from Catholic bishops and nobility. In January 1547 they were in disarray. Gardiner, bishop of Winchester, their principal spokesman, had fallen out of favour with Henry and was excluded from the council; and Norfolk, the leading Catholic peer, was in the Tower on a charge of treason. Without papal guidance or any sign that princess Mary, a devout Catholic, would fight their corner, conservative bishops like Bonner, Tunstall, Heath and Gardiner, could only resist the changes passively. They opposed the reforms in convocation and avoided confrontation for as long as possible until their consciences and the reforming régime forced them to resign.

b) The Main Religious Changes

As the new administration secured its political hold in 1547, it was understandably reluctant to embark on religious reforms which might destabilise the country. Most people were Catholic and it would take some time to persuade them to accept changes to their beliefs and customs. In May Cranmer issued an English *Book of Homilies* to improve the quality of preaching and urged his clergy to desist from practising traditional customs. Creeping to the cross, ringing bells for the dead and using holy water and candles to ward off evil spirits were, in his view, 'ungodly and counterfeit religion', and were to stop. Episcopal visitations were ordered to ensure that ministers read sermons from the *Homilies* at least four times a year and they had to possess a copy of Erasmus's *Paraphrases* on the Gospels. Such reforms continued Cranmer's work that had been halted in 1538 and were the opening round in his attack on the Catholic faith.

The first legislative acts of reform began in the winter of 1547. The Act of Six Articles, Treason Act and *De Heretico Comburendo* (which authorised the burning of heretics) were abolished and a Chantry Act passed. Masses for the dead were thus ended and the doctrine of purgatory, which underpinned their foundation, was denied. The motive behind this dissolution of chantry chapels was principally theological but the government also benefited from seizing the lands which had endowed them worth £25,000 a year and acquired church plate, bells and ornaments at a time of financial crisis. The impact of the loss of the chantries was momentous: every English church had one or more lights at a side altar, ornaments donated by parishioners and property locally endowed for priests to say masses for dead relatives. All this now ended. Surprisingly, there was very little open resistance to the commissioners who arrived in 1548 to close the chapels down and seize their assets – the archdeacon of Cornwall and four people in Yorkshire were murdered – but there was considerable non-cooperation from parishioners as they tried successfully to conceal fabric and ornaments, as well as property, from the government agents.

Many areas of the country showed little support for reform and, in the case of Winchester and Durham, the bishops refused to conduct services in English. Conversely, in Kent, Essex and London, the opportunity to implement reforms was seized with enthusiasm. Indeed, reports in 1548 of shouting and quarrelling in church, of priests being mobbed by crowds, and of acts of iconoclasm – chalices, pyxes and candlesticks were desecrated, church walls whitewashed and images stolen – alarmed the government. And fear that, once started, a popular reformation would be difficult to stop, explains a series of proclamations that were issued in 1548 and 1549. In the meantime, Cranmer was working with Bucer to produce an English prayer book which was finally published in June 1549. It contained all the services required by a priest and combined traditional English prayers – matins, mass and evensong based on the *Sarum Use* – with services used in Cologne, Nuremberg and other reformed German cities. Indeed the services for baptism and confirmation owed much to the church orders written by Melanchthon and Bucer. While the prayer book may be described as a compromise, and Bucer was particularly critical of its conservatism, it was nevertheless a clear rejection of many traditional practices. Gone was anointing at confirmation, confession became optional and both bread and wine were to be made available at communion as an act of remembrance. No longer were there to be processions, daily masses, or the elevation of the host, and gone from the calendar were most of the holy days – all that remained were Christmas, Easter and Whitsun.

An Act of Uniformity established a series of fines and punishments for anyone who refused to use the prayer book but there was no penalty for non-attendance at church. Although eight bishops opposed the book in convocation, very few clergy were subsequently deprived of their livings. The only serious opposition came from Devon and Cornwall where a rebellion broke out on Whit Monday 1549. These protesters considered the new services 'lyke a Christmas game', and called for all English prayers and the Bible to be abolished and for monasteries, chantries, the Latin mass and traditional customs to be restored. This Western Rebellion was partly motivated by social and economic concerns but really reflected the views of a deeply conservative area of England which wanted orthodox Catholicism without papal rule. Much smaller disturbances occurred in Yorkshire, Oxfordshire, Buckinghamshire and Hampshire, but the government stood firm and the new prayer book remained.

Under the administration of Northumberland (formerly the earl of Warwick), further reforms occurred that brought England even closer to the continental Reformation. Bucer helped Cranmer prepare a new Ordinal which required bishops at ordinations to preach the Gospel in English and to stress that the mass was not a sacrificial act on behalf of the living. A new bench of bishops brought changes to London, Exeter, Norwich, Durham, Chichester and Rochester, and in 1551 to Worcester and Gloucester. These men were keen to implement reform and more than cooperated with royal commissioners who surveyed parishes again and seized superfluous church goods. Undoubtedly the highwater mark of this second wave of evangelical reform was Cranmer's revised prayer book of 1552. It owed a great deal to Ridley and Martyr and was far more Zwinglian than the 1549 book. Images and side altars were to be removed and a high altar replaced by a movable wooden table placed at the centre of the church. The minister was to stand in the north transept and, wearing a plain white surplice and none of the traditional vestments, he was to offer communion as an act of remembrance using household bread and wine. There was to be no signing of the cross at confirmation or exorcism at baptism, no kneeling at communion or blessing of the ring in marriage. Cranmer had wanted to retain these last two rituals but was outvoted in convocation by more Calvinist orientated bishops like Knox, Hooper and Latimer. To Cranmer, whether or not to outlaw these features was unimportant or 'adiaphora', but to radicals it was essential. An Act of Uniformity enforced much stiffer penalties than before both for non-compliance and for non-attendance. There were no subsequent rebellions or executions but life imprisonment was the penalty meted out to Bonner, Tunstall, Day, Heath and Gardiner when they refused to use the book.

When Cranmer prepared 42 Articles as a comprehensive statement of faith in June 1553, England was a Protestant country at least in theory. Most bishops and parish clergy had implemented the reforms: some changes, such as the introduction of clerical marriage, had been warmly received; others, like the confiscation of church plate and ornaments in 1552, had been deeply resented. Crown officials, gentry and merchants, who bought monastic and chantry land, had a vested interest in preserving the Reformation whether or not they agreed with the doctrinal changes. In general, the south and east of England, especially London, Kent and Essex, set the pace of change and often marched ahead of the rest of the country. Their churchwardens' accounts reveal that images and vestments were removed, walls were white washed, rood screens cut down, stone altars smashed, and the king's arms and the Ten Commandments portrayed in place of the rood. Elsewhere there was only lukewarm support for reform and positive resistance in some counties such as Lancashire, Cornwall and Durham. Here, items were stolen, removed or concealed. Ridley was right when he later reported that most Englishmen 'were never persuaded in their hearts, but from the teeth forward and for the king's sake, in the truth of God's Word'.[2] When Edward died in July 1553, it would not take his Catholic successor long to repeal the Protestant legislation.

3 The Marian Reformation, 1553–58

> **KEY ISSUES** How did Mary and her advisers try to restore England to its traditional Catholicism? How effective were they by 1558?

At her accession, Mary had three principal religious objectives: to return the English Church and the ex-monastic and chantry lands back to the papacy; to remove heresy and enforce Catholic orthodoxy; and to improve standards of preaching, pastoral care and clerical morality. These were not impossible aims and most carried the support of her people, many of whom looked forward to a return to traditional ways. Parliament would, of course, need to be called to reverse existing legislation but Mary envisaged few difficulties. Indeed, she believed that the Protestant reforms had been the work of a misguided minority of theologians backed by Edward's councillors and, once these people had been removed, a Catholic restoration would follow.

The queen and her principal adviser, Reginald Pole, who returned to London from Rome in November 1554, have often been seen as narrow-minded, out-of-touch, and lacking in imagination as they set about re-building the Catholic faith. After all, Mary had a pessimistic view of religious conditions in England and seriously under-estimated the degree to which many areas had become attached to Protestantism. Pole, on the other hand, had been out of the country for 20 years and preferred to work with the clergy rather than the laity who, he should have realised, held the purse strings of church patronage. Between them, it is often argued, they misjudged their audience and mishandled their mission. Yet, in reality, their strategy was sound. Slowly and surely they would revive the Catholic Church, not by putting the clock back to the 1520s but by introducing a blend of new and traditional ideas suitable for the 1550s.

Before the end of 1553, Mary had released Catholic bishops from prison, deprived evangelical bishops and deported foreign preachers and refugees. Parliament had repealed all of Edward's reforms and restored the Latin services, the orthodox mass and the Act of Six Articles of 1539. So far so good, but already some MPs were demurring at restoring papal supremacy, monastic lands and punishments for non-attendance at church. For the moment, Mary let matters rest; she had made a good start and would wait for the return to England of cardinal Pole. Early in 1554, however, the queen stiffened her attitude towards non-conformists. All married clergy were told to give up their wives or resign their livings; Mary did not agree with clerical marriage. In the course of the year, some 2,000 clergy were dismissed; one-third of all benefices in London alone were empty by Easter. Mary and her bishops then turned to the advocates of evangelicalism. Cranmer, Ridley, Latimer, Hooper, Coverdale and Rogers were imprisoned for refusing to celebrate mass and nearly all heads of Cambridge colleges were sacked. Already there was a steady stream of Protestants leaving for the continent. Soon it became a flood. By 1558 more than 800 'Marian exiles', mainly merchants, students, clerics and gentry, had fled abroad. Undoubtedly the mood of the country became more sombre when Spanish theologians arrived with Philip II and received university and royal positions. Villagarcia and de Soto, Dominican monks, were installed at Oxford; and Carranza, who became Mary's confessor, and de Castro, remained in London.

It was the triumphant return of Pole in 1554 which had the greatest impact in effecting Mary's religious plans. As the papal legate, Pole granted absolution to the country and accepted parliament's apology for the 'schism and disobedience committed in this realm'. Some MPs and peers, including Gardiner, had reservations about acknowledging the pope's authority but Mary was insistent. There was similar unease when the question of recovering church lands was broached. The impracticality of this idea – most land had been sold and subsequent re-sales could not be traced easily – and the great personal loss to MPs that such a proposal entailed made it implausible. In 1555 Pole conceded defeat and accepted £60,000 a year in compensation and in lieu of papal taxes. This, however, would never be enough to revitalise the Church. Indeed the shortage of church finances was always a serious limitation, perhaps far more than Pole appreciated. For example, every encouragement was given to refound monasteries and chantries, and restorations occurred at Westminster, Sheen, Syon and Greenwich, but attempts elsewhere ended in failure.

In December 1554 Mary informed her council: 'Touching punishment of heretics, we think it ought to be done without rashness, not leaving in the meanwhile to do justice to such as by learning would seem to deceive the simple.' She had been disappointed at the slowness of the Catholic restoration and the persistence of Protestants. Both the queen and Pole were convinced that the persecution of a minority was necessary so that the people 'shall both understand the truth and beware to do the like'. Gardiner, Bonner and Philip initially agreed, although doubts were soon raised about the effectiveness of burning heretics. Parliament, in fact, only agreed to re-introduce the death penalty in 1555 when the pope confirmed that he would not attempt to re-possess monastic land. Between 1555 and 1558, some 280 Protestants were burned at the stake. 85 per cent came from the east and south-east – a product of bishop Bonner's enthusiasm – and were mainly weavers, craftsmen and people of humble birth. There were also some distinguished martyrs, bishops Cranmer, Ridley, Latimer and Hooper among them. If there had been 'widespread indifference' towards Protestantism before the persecution, as David Loades suggests, there was growing sympathy and support for the victims as a result. A crowd of some 7,000 allegedly turned up at Gloucester to pray for Hooper and an abundance of adverse propaganda flooded England from the continent. Some of it condemned the Catholic faith, such as Christopher Goodman's *How superior powers ought to be obeyed*; some attacked Spaniards, like John Ponet's *Short treatise of Politike Power*; and some railed against female rulers, like John Knox's *The First Blast of the Trumpet Against the Monstrous Regiment of Women*.

Historians have been perhaps understandably drawn towards the burnings as the centre-piece of the Marian Reformation and have underplayed Pole's and Bonner's success in improving the moral and spiritual condition of the laity and the clergy. Both recognised the need to educate the laity to understand the meaning behind Catholic rituals, to explain the ceremonies and to counter reformist ideas, and so prove the validity of the sacraments. To do this, the clergy were instructed to preach every holy day, to catechise the young and to demonstrate the beauty of holiness. Of course, the clergy needed assistance and, to this effect, seminaries were to be established in every diocese and grammar schools in every town. Bonner produced the *Profytable and necessary doctryne . . . for the instruction and enformation of the people*, a book containing traditional prayers and doctrine, and his chaplain wrote a set of 13 *Homilies* to help the less competent clergy. In addition, a revised edition of the New Testament and a Primer in English with a Latin version in the margin were printed in 1555. Bonner also drew up a programme of visitations and first introduced it in his London diocese. Priests answered questions concerning their education, teaching, marital status, residence and knowledge of Protestantism, and every church was ordered to possess vestments, copes, ornaments, bells, prayer books, a high altar, a rood, images to saints, lights and side altars.

Pole and Bonner worked hard to reform Catholicism and make the ritual and ceremonies relevant to the people. But what had been achieved by 1558? On balance, historians have claimed that a great deal of harm and very little good was accomplished. No seminary was established in Mary's lifetime and only a handful of schools and colleges; several parishes were without an incumbent due to the shortage of unmarried and acceptable priests; the papacy was restored in name but not in sentiment; and the decision to burn heretics had proved disastrous. Revisionist historians, however, point out that the period saw many initiatives, some of which bore fruit in Elizabeth's reign and, had it not been for inadequate finance and insufficient time, Pole's policies could have succeeded. John Jewel, on his return from exile in 1559, would probably have agreed. He commented on the Catholic activity in Oxford of the two Spanish theologians, de Soto and Villagarcia, who 'have so torn up by the roots all that Peter Martyr had so prosperously planted'.[3] Nicholas Harpsfield, archdeacon of Canterbury, reported in 1557 that even in Kent most parishes had met the requirements laid down by Bonner, although many had no lamp burning before the Sacrament and few had the full set of vestments, altar cloths and ornaments. This picture of a partial Catholic restoration has been borne out by Ronald Hutton's study of 134 extant churchwardens' accounts for 1558.[4] Most reveal genuine attempts by parishes to equip their churches with traditional materials. Many experienced difficulties in getting workmen to rebuild altars, belfries and lofts, or in procuring texts; and a lot retrieved confiscated goods or planned to obtain them in the future. Unfortunately, there was to be no future. On 17 November 1558 Mary died, and the Catholic Reformation died with her.

4 The Elizabethan Reformation, 1558-71

> **KEY ISSUES** What was the nature of the Church Settlement? What was the condition of the Church of England by 1571?

a) The Elizabethan Church Settlement of 1559

No one could be sure how the English Church would be affected by the new Elizabethan régime. The queen had been educated by Protestants and was known to dislike the Catholic mass yet she had a personal liking for traditional ceremonies and an aversion for extremes. The Marian bishops, of course, favoured the 'status quo' but this was out of the question. Elizabeth intended resuming the supremacy of the Church and ending the persecution of heretics, both of which ensured her lasting popularity. While the Catholic bias in her council could be redressed, it was prudent to keep an even-handed approach since England could ill-afford to alienate either Catholic France or Spain. Moreover, at the outset of her reign, Elizabeth hoped at least to retain the friendship of the pope to secure her own legitimacy. Parliament, on the other hand, would prove more difficult to manage. The Lords contained a large number of Catholics and the Commons would be influenced by a small but determined minority of zealous reformers, encouraged by Marian exiles returning from the continent. On balance, most people wanted continuity rather than change and had no wish to return to the excesses of Edwardian Protestantism and Marian Catholicism.

Elizabeth hoped to accomplish any changes as quietly and quickly as possible. Advised by Cecil, Bacon and Aylmer, the queen firstly banned all preaching outside the royal court to prevent idle speculation and then, in 1559, invited parliament to pass a bill of supremacy. When arguments arose and doctrinal issues were discussed, she turned to her theologians and convened a meeting at Westminster. They, too, argued and the bishops Lincoln and Winchester were sent to the Tower for their obduracy. Finally, in April parliament was called upon to draft two bills of supremacy and uniformity that would constitute the Church settlement. The Act of Supremacy was skilfully phrased to allow all groups to subscribe to it without compromising their faith or conscience. The queen would be the 'Supreme Governor of the Church of England in all things ecclesiastical as well as temporal'. Far more contentious was the Act of Uniformity. It contained details of the content and order of Church services to be embodied in a new prayer book. Many MPs favoured the Edwardian book of 1552 and were supported by Marian exiles like Richard Cox, recently returned from Frankfurt. A minority of exiles wanted to adopt the more radical Genevan prayer book, while conservatives in the Lords hoped that, if they could not have a Catholic book, then at least they could insist on the 1549 book which had combined Protestant and Catholic practices. Amid bitter debates and several amendments, a bill was narrowly passed that reflected a sensible compromise. Communion was to be celebrated with bread and wine but the official meaning of the Eucharist was kept deliberately vague. When the minister offered the bread, he was to say in English:

> The body of our Lord Jesus Christ, which was given for thee, preserve thy body and soul unto everlasting life [1549 edition]: and take and eat this in remembrance that Christ died for thee, and feed on him in thine heart by faith, with thanksgiving [1552 edition].

The minister then delivered the chalice of wine saying:

> The blood of our Lord Jesus Christ, which was shed for thee, preserve thy body and soul unto everlasting life [1549]: and drink this in remembrance that Christ's blood was shed for thee, and be thankful [1552].

Traditional rituals, however, which were to be found in the 1549 book and in Catholic manuals, remained at least 'until other order shall be therin taken'. The queen had no wish to preside over a Zwinglian or Calvinist church, but radical Protestants were encouraged by this statement. Bowing at the name of Jesus, kneeling at communion and blessing the ring in marriage were retained, as were clerical vestments. Although Elizabeth did not believe the clergy should marry, it was once again permitted and proved a popular decision. Finally, the heresy laws were repealed and in their place was a one shilling fine (5p) a week for anyone who failed to attend services on Sundays and holy days. As the queen confirmed, 'she wished to open windows into no man's soul'. Provided her subjects outwardly conformed to her settlement, she would be content.

Further details were set out in royal injunctions later in 1559 to establish clerical uniformity. All churches were to have a copy of Erasmus's *Paraphrases*, a *Primer*, and the English Bible. Every cleric was to teach children the Ten Commandments and Lord's Prayer, and all preachers were to be licensed. Finally, it was made clear that all images, lights, roods, side altars and chantries were unnecessary for salvation and must be removed. Music, however, would continue because the queen liked it. In 1563 convocation published 38 articles re-affirming the settlement but no mention was made of the Eucharist. When parliament finally endorsed these articles in 1571, it rectified this and the 39 Articles became the basis of the Anglican faith. Together with the Act of Supremacy and an oath defending the prayer book, these remained the Church's essential tests for conformity for the next 250 years.

b) The Condition of the Church in 1571

One of the unique features of the English Reformation was the authority exercised by the bishops. On the continent they had been replaced by pastors, elders and ministers, and the governing body (convocation) had been supplanted by a synod. Not so in England. Elizabeth, like her Tudor predecessors, depended upon her bishops as administrators, advisers and enforcers of her laws. They were in effect crown servants, appointed by and subject to the queen; they were vital to the maintenance of uniformity and order in both civil and ecclesiastical affairs. In 1559 all but one of the surviving Marian bishops resigned, and this undoubtedly eased the transition from Catholicism to Protestantism. Matthew Parker, who was a moderate reformer and well known to the queen (he had been her mother's chaplain), was appointed archbishop of Canterbury. In the course of the next year, the queen assisted by Parker and William Cecil, her principal secretary, filled the vacant bishoprics with divines many of whom had been in exile: Grindal, formerly of Strasbourg, went to London; Jewel of Zurich to Salisbury; and Cox of Frankfurt to Ely. Notably those bishops who had been to Geneva were out of favour with the queen.

Apart from some 300 beneficed clergy, the vast majority of clergy accepted the changes and continued in office. This was most reassuring for the queen and her government. However, some benefices were difficult to fill. Vacancies remained well into the 1560s and the bishops of Gloucester and Norwich reported that they had to allow pluralism to continue. Less pleasing was the growing demand in many parishes to rid the prayer book of its Catholic traditions. This pressure surfaced in 1563 when the lower house of convocation debated a series of proposals to end the use of vestments, church music, holy days and similar customs, and was only defeated by one vote. Parker may well have sympathised with the reformers but was obliged by the queen to take a firm stand against further change. Indeed, by revoking all licences for preaching and suspending 37 clerics, he was able to stop the reformers from using convocation as a means of changing the settlement. These 'hotter sort of Protestants', contemporarily known as Puritans, turned their attention to other methods of achieving their goal and presented a serious challenge to the Church after 1571 (see Chapter 7). They believed that the Elizabethan Church was only 'half-reformed' and did not represent a radical enough break with the past.

English Catholics, in contrast, spent the 1560s in introspection. The pope gave no guidance as to how they should proceed until 1566 when he told them not to attend church services, and the Catholic nobility showed no desire to challenge the queen. Some Catholics went abroad and returned later in the reign strengthened by their contacts wiith seminary priests and Jesuits. The arrival in the north of England in 1568 of Mary, Queen of Scots, completely changed the situation. She was heir presumptive to the English throne and a devout Roman Catholic. Within a year of her arrival, she had inspired a rebellion of nobles (Westmoreland, Northumberland, Dacre and Norfolk), triggered the pope to excommunicate Elizabeth and encouraged an Italian Ridolfi to plot to kill the queen. By 1571 anti-Catholic sentiment in the council and parliament had reached such a pitch that additional penalties were imposed upon anyone who refused to attend church (they would have their goods seized) and anyone found in possession of papal relics (they would be executed). It had not been the queen's wish to legislate against either Puritans or Catholics. She wanted to rule a country, not lead a party, yet from 1571 Catholics would be watched and harassed, fines for recusancy (non-attendance) would be more rigorously collected and the country would begin to identify Protestantism with patriotism.

Evidence from churchwardens' accounts and visitation records indicate the limited enthusiasm with which many parishes greeted reform. Widespread concealment of images, ornaments and vestments were reported in Exeter, Chester, York and London. The bishop of Lichfield and Coventry in 1565 had to urge 'the people daily that they cast away their beads with all their superstitions that they do use'.[5] A survey of the diocese of Chichester in 1569 reported little interest in reform and images were concealed 'ready to be set up again'. There were similar reports from Shropshire, Lincolnshire and Lancashire. Priests in Sussex kept their old chalices 'looking for to have mass again' and at Durham altar stones, which had been taken down, were hidden in a quarry and re-erected in the cathedral during the 1569 rebellion. In fact, many Marian vicars and clerics of a conservative outlook remained in office because Elizabeth had no great desire to see them removed. There was a shortage of graduate and competent preachers and the strategy of slowly absorbing Catholics into conformity seemed the most pragmatic course of action to adopt. As far as the queen was concerned, to be effective the Reformation must of necessity be a slow, gradual process of change.

Summary Diagram
'The English Reformation'

Principal Religious Changes (1534–71)

Henry VIII	Break from Rome (1534)
+	Act of 10 Articles (1536)
Cranmer	Dissolution of the Monasteries (1536–9)
	English Bible (1539)
	Act of Six Articles (1539)
Edward VI	Repeal of the Six Articles (1547)
+	Dissolution of the chantries (1547)
Cranmer	First English Prayer Book (1549)
	Second Prayer Book (1552)
	Act of 42 Articles (1553)
Mary I	Act of Six Articles restored (1553)
+	Papal relations restored (1554)
Pole	Protestant burnings began (1555)
Elizabeth I	Act of Supremacy (1559)
+	Act of Uniformity repealed Six Articles (1559)
Parker	Excommunication of Elizabeth (1570)
	Act of 39 Articles (1571)

Footnotes

1. D. MacCulloch, *Tudor Church Militant* (Allen Lane, 2000).
2. J. Foxe, *Acts and Monuments*, vi, p. 678.
3. H. Robinson (ed.), *Zurich Letters* (Parker Society,1842), i, p. 33.
4. R. Hutton,'The Local Impact of the Tudor Reformation' in C.A. Haigh (ed), *The English Reformation Revised* (C.U.P., 1987), pp. 114–38.
5. E. Duffy, *The Stripping of the Altars* (Yale U. P., 1992), p. 572.

Answering structured questions on Chapter 5

The following are typical AS questions:
a) How far was the church in England in need of reform in 1529?
b) What was the nature of the Henrician Reform in 1529–47?
c) How far was England a Protestant country by 1553?
d) How much popular support was there for the various religious changes between 1553 and 1571?

Answering coursework questions on Chapter 5

The A Level History specifications have a compulsory coursework module which allows you to research a subject of your own choice. The English Reformation is an ideal quarry for a personal study, but how do you set about this task? Two principal decisions need to be taken: do you want to investigate an in-depth or broad-based subject, and do you have the opportunity to use primary as well as secondary source material? First, you should decide whether you wish to study a regional or national theme. In each case you will need to consider how the Reformation brought about change over a period of time and discuss any similarities and differences which accompanied these changes. This will enable you to make comparative judgements and identify turning-points in the history of the English Reformation. Regional studies work well because you can draw upon material which is both specific to a diocese or county and can be contrasted with other areas of the country. Thus a study of how two counties were affected by the dissolution of the monasteries will provide you with the opportunity to compare religious, social and economic changes. An investigation into land ownership brought about by the secularisation of monastic, chantry and episcopal lands will enable you to compare patterns of ownership before and after the Reformation.

Popular with many students are studies centred upon a prominent ecclesiastic, someone who played a key role in the development of the Reformation. Suitable subjects for research are Wolsey, Cranmer, Gardiner, Pole, Bonner and Parker, and a consideration of their aims, problems, successes and failures would be possible lines of investigation. Equally viable would be a study of two periods that experienced contrasting religious changes: how and why, for example, did the Church of England change so much in the reigns of Edward and Mary? Thematic studies are usually best examined with reference to the national picture. If, for instance, you want to look at the social impact of the Reformation in England, then you will find it easier and more fruitful to draw examples from a range of regions across the country. Similarly, a study of religious rebellions can demonstrate popular reactions to doctrinal and ecclesiastical reforms (as well as other issues) but needs to be set in a national context. The Reformation occurred over a period of time and the more that you can show the variety of developments, the stronger your study will be. For example, an investigation into the impact of the Reformation on bishops, monks, chantry priests and parish clergy over 30 or so years and for different areas of the country would work well.

Second, you must consider the resources at your disposal and whether you are well placed to conduct your own research. Reformation studies are not as simple as they may appear at first sight. For almost all AS and A Level students, a study of primary sources will depend on whether you can easily visit your county record office, university and local libraries. Many documents concerning the English Reformation have been printed, at least in a calendared or edited form, and these are likely to be the basis of your research. Wills, churchwardens' accounts, diocesan records, chantry certificates, monastic surveys and sales of church property are all suitable evidence for an A Level piece of coursework. If you have limited opportunities to visit your local and county record offices and cannot afford the expense of inter-library loans, you will need to resort to secondary sources and use the extracts and collection of primary documents which many contain. In recent years there have been some excellent studies on local, regional and national topics, as well as biographies of Reformation figures and the on-going historiographical debate. All studies should demonstrate that you have looked at a range of sources and that you have understood the changes brought about by the Reformation in the course of the sixteenth century.

6 The Catholic Reformation

POINTS TO CONSIDER

In the course of the sixteenth century, the Catholic Church took a long, hard look at itself in an attempt to stop countries from defecting to the Protestant cause. This chapter examines the main features of the reformed Catholic Church – the new orders, the Council of Trent, the Inquisition and Index, and the revitalised papacy. But just how far was the Catholic Reformation merely a reaction to the Protestant challenge? And were institutional changes or the contribution of individuals the real driving force behind the movement?

KEY DATES

1524	Order of Theatines established in Rome.
1528	Capuchins founded in Ancona.
1530	Barnabites established in Milan.
1532	Ursulines founded in Brescia.
1537	Report published on the abuses in the curia.
1540	Paul III recognised the Society of Jesus.
1542	Roman Inquisition began.
1545–9	First session of the Council of Trent.
1551–2	Second session of the Council of Trent.
1559	Paul IV published the first Roman Index.
1562–3	Third session of the Council of Trent.
1565	Archbishop Borromeo began reforms in Milan.
1572	Gregory XIII improved the city of Rome.
1588	Reorganisation of papal administration under Sixtus V.

1 Early Catholic Reform Movements

KEY ISSUES What reforms took place before 1540? Were they mainly in response to the Protestant Reformation?

a) Pre-Lutheran Reforms

We suggested in Chapter 2 that both head and members of the Roman Catholic Church recognised the need to implement reforms many years before Luther rose to prominence. Fifteenth-century church councils (at Basle and Florence) had initiated reform programmes in the 1430s and 1440s and emphasised the value of having a resident clergy if pastoral and sacramental duties were to be properly fulfilled. Some popes like Eugenius IV and Nicholas V led by example and embodied the prevailing mood of devotional piety. Some monastic orders, notably in Spain and France, dissatisfied with the lax ways enjoyed by conventuals, returned to more orthodox practices and refounded observant orders. Dominican and Franciscan friars on the other hand stressed the value of preaching and dispensed with choral recitation so as to spend more time in the community. Secular groups also provided opportunities for the laity to perform charitable work, and oratories were established in Genoa and Rome for this purpose. Episcopal reforms were evident in most European countries where humanist scholars, bishops and cardinals sought to improve the quality of the clergy and so meet the growing demand for more (and better) Christian instruction. Between 1474 and 1516, Isabella and Ferdinand of Spain had demonstrated what could be achieved: Isabella rejected the idea of tolerating non-Christian groups in Castile and began a remorseless campaign against heretics – first Muslims and then Jews – and set up the Spanish Inquisition to prevent any backsliding into apostasy. Bishops, like Talavera and Ximenes, were encouraged to reform monasteries, improve the overall level of clerical training and with it the spiritual condition of the laity. It was during this period that the foundations of the Catholic Reformation in Spain were laid.

There was, however, a feeling at the turn of the century that still more could and should be done to improve the condition of the Church. Cardinal Giles Viterbo warned delegates at the opening of the Lateran council in 1512 that 'unless by the council or by some other means we place a limit on our morals, unless we force our greedy desire for human things, the source of evils, to yield to the love of divine things, it is all over with Christendom'.[1] By 1517 the Roman ecclesiastics had concurred that priests must begin to live chastely, that simony should be outlawed, and that preachers must be competent and suitable in their integrity, age, knowledge, prudence and exemplary life. To these Italian cardinals and Pope Leo X, the people deserved better spiritual guidance and the way to head off potential critics was to reform the clerical abuses. These were noble words but the quality of recent popes and the college of cardinals who elected them left much to be desired. Simony, pluralism, nepotism and absenteeism ran through the papal curia, and every papal candidate since 1471 had promised to call a general council to remedy the ills; but none had. The Catholic Church therefore knew what it had to do and a spirit of reform was already in the air in 1517, but it still lacked a sense of urgency and leadership. Indeed, even after Luther's double-headed attack on papal supremacy and orthodox theology, only in 1545 did a general council meet to address these and other matters raised by the Protestant Reformation. Why did it take so long to convene, and what progress did the Church make in these years to put its own house in order?

b) Reform Initiatives

The tragedy of the Reformation as far as Catholics were concerned was the slow and ineffectual way in which the papacy responded to

Luther and to subsequent Protestant heretics. On the face of it, and given that both institutional and governmental reforms existed before Protestantism had established a foothold, it is surprising to find that not until the pontificate of Paul III (1534–49) did the papacy really respond to the challenge. Two reasons probably account for this delay – poor quality popes and the impact of the Italian wars. Most popes between 1517 and 1534 were more interested in Italian politics and the welfare of their own family fortunes. Leo X (1513–21), for example, was well versed in selling church offices and was unable to change the ingrained habits of his curia. He did what he could to silence Luther but ultimately relied upon German secular authoriities to carry out his bull of excommunication. Adrian VI (1521–23) was fully aware of the need to combat Luther and unite Christian princes against the advancing Turks, as first Belgrade and then Rhodes fell to them, but he died within 20 months of taking office. His successor, Clement VII (1523–34), was far too easy-going and, in the opinion of contemporaries, talked about reform but never really intended summoning a council. Even the sack of Rome by drunken imperial troops in 1527 failed to shake him out of his lethargy. He distrusted general councils and was supported by curial officials fearful of what reforms might do to their privileged position.

The dynastic conflict between Charles V and Francis I, which was being played out in Italy, also prevented the Catholic Church from focusing upon the common enemy. Italian cardinals and popes had good reason to distrust foreign princes whose armies continued to wage war in northern Italy. Charles V's troops not only looted Rome, they took the pope prisoner. So why should Clement help the emperor solve his Lutheran problem? As for Francis I of France, who contested Charles' control of Naples and Milan, he was seen as a fair-weather friend. He tolerated humanist and Lutheran influences at home and opened discussions with the Turks abroad, such was his cynical opportunism and uncertain religious disposition. Henry VIII seemed little better. Although he was no friend of Lutherans, the king also dabbled in Italian politics and, of course, broke from Rome when he tried without success to obtain a divorce.

Changes occurred with the accession of Paul III in 1534. While his own life-style was akin to his Renaissance predecessors – he blatantly advanced members of his own Farnese family – he was willing to support a growing number of Italian cardinals keen to initiate reforms. In 1536 he commissioned a report on clerical abuses which made unpleasant reading. It painted a picture of absentee bishops and cardinals, corrupt monks and priests, and low quality preaching. One of the commissioners was Giberti, bishop of Verona (1527–43), who had already begun to improve standards of preaching in his diocese, provided poor relief for the sick and homeless, and had a reputation as a disciplinarian. Giberti was one of several bishops – others were Sadoleto, Carafa and Contarini – who were in contact as to how best to reform the Church. In 1542

Carafa was instrumental in establishing a Roman Inquisition and Contarini was a keen supporter of the *spirituali*, Catholic evangelicals who believed that preaching was the key to combatting Lutheranism and safeguarding people's souls. In fact, by stressing the role of the individual and the importance of justification by faith, the *spirituali* shared some of Luther's theological ideas and genuinely believed that a reconciliation between Catholics and Protestants was attainable.

Charles V had long hoped for an end to the schism in Germany and endorsed a series of conferences between 1539 and 1542 to this end. One such meeting took place in Regensburg in 1541 when Catholic and Protestant theologians met with Contarini, the pope's emissary. It was a historic conference and seemed most promising. Melanchthon, the Lutheran spokesman, agreed with Contarini on a definition of 'double justification' – that justification can be inherited at birth but, if man was to be saved, then he must also acquire divine justification by good works. Unfortunately, no agreement was reached on the sacraments or the authority of the Church and when the delegates returned home, even the consensus on justification by faith was denounced by Luther and the pope. The emperor was now convinced that only a general council of the Church could resolve the Lutheran problem and, of course, clerical abuses would be high on the council's agenda. Peace still had to be reached between Charles and Francis but when this was achieved in 1544, at least temporarily, the way was clear for a council to meet at Trent, selected because it was geographically in Italy but politically under the emperor's jurisdiction. In practice neither France nor the Lutherans would send any delegates to the opening session but this was a minor consideration to Paul III, the mainly Italian delegates, and perhaps even Charles V, who were all anxious to heal the schism caused by the Protestant Reformation.

c) The New Orders

A distinctive feature of the Catholic Reformation was the emergence of several new religious orders in Italy during this period. They were not founded to counter Protestantism but to meet the social and ecclesiastical needs of the people whose living conditions had worsened as armies devastated much of central and northern Italy in the 1520s.

- In 1524 cardinals Carafa and Cajetan founded the Theatines in Rome, a brotherhood pledged to work in hospitals, preaching and praying, and which relied totally on charitable endowments.
- Four years later, Franciscan friars established the Capuchins in Ancona. Dedicated to a life of poverty and preaching, they were initially confined to Italy and established some 300 convents with over 3,500 members by 1574. Therafter, the order spread to France, Spain, the Netherlands and Germany, and its numbers had doubled by the end of the century.

- Another charitable order was the 'Society of Servants of the Poor', founded in 1531, and better known as the Somaschi, a town near Venice. This small organisation was dedicated to working among orphans, prostitutes and the poor.
- Two years later, Antonio Zaccaria founded the Barnabites in Milan. Their aim was to raise the moral condition of the clergy and commoners by working in prisons and hospitals and so setting a standard that others might follow. The Barnabites spread slowly to nine other Italian cities in the course of the sixteenth century.
- Two charities run by women began in the 1530s. The Ursulines were established by Angela Merici in Brescia to look after orphans, assist in hospitals and educate girls in the Christian doctrine. Some of the women lived in a convent, others at home, and their numbers steadily grew: there were 35 members in 1535, 150 four years later, and by 1584 some 600 sisters ran 18 schools. By then the order of nuns had been confined to convents but their life of prayer, self-denial and charity had acquired an international standing and convents were set up in France and the Spanish Netherlands in the early seventeenth century.
- Finally, the Angelica were established in Milan, as a female counterpart to the Barnabites. Initially they worked and prayed with the monks before being segregated and placed under male discipline. Each of these new orders, as teachers, preachers and pastoral workers, demonstrated a keenness to help the less fortunate and followed in the footsteps of fifteenth-century clerics, confraternities and lay charities.

2 Loyola and the Jesuits

KEY ISSUES What were the main characteristics of the Jesuits? What had they achieved by 1600?

-Profile-

IGNATIUS LOYOLA

Born into a noble Basque family in 1491, Loyola served as a soldier in the Spanish army until he was seriously wounded in 1521. During his convalescence, he had a vision and decided to devote his life to God. He went on a pilgrimage to Montserrat, then lived as a hermit for nine months, before visiting the Holy Land in 1523. On his return he studied at Alcalá, Salamanca and Paris universities. In August 1534, he and six friends vowed to convert all

> Moslems to Christianity but war made it impossible to reach Jerusalem. Instead they went to Rome, were joined by three more supporters, and pledged their lives in the service of the pope. Paul III gave them specific tasks to accomplish, such as social work in Ischia, monastic reform in Siena and pastoral duties in Parma, before formally registering their order as the Society of Jesus in 1540. Loyola, its first general, spent the rest of his life in Rome where he died in 1556.

a) Loyola's Ideas

The Jesuits were the best known of the new religious orders. Like other recent foundations, they were not formed to combat Protestantism but to 'help souls' although their intention to 'propagate the faith' soon brought them into conflict with Protestant preachers and pastoral workers. Indeed, ten years after their foundation, the revised *Formula of the Institute* spoke of the 'defence and propagation of the faith' as its main aim. In 1559 when the *Constitutions of the Society* were first published, the aims and role of the Jesuits had considerably expanded. They encompassed:

1 Public preaching, lectures, and any other ministrations whatsoever of the word of God, and further by means of the *Spiritual Exercises*, the education of children and unlettered persons in Christianity, and the spiritual consolation of Christ's faithful through hearing confessions and
5 administering the other sacraments. Moreover, the Society should show itself no less useful in reconciling the estranged, in holily asserting and serving those who are found in prisons and hospitals, and indeed in performing any other works of charity, according to what will seem expedient for the glory of God and the common good.[2]

Unlike Luther, Loyola saw the reform of the individual rather than theological or institutional reform as the key to the Church's renewal. Heavily influenced by medieval mysticism, especially the works of Kempis, Loyola devised a series of meditative prayers, questions and commentaries, known as *Spiritual Exercises*, which offered the student advice and guidance. Intended to be followed over a four-week period, this programme of self-evaluation progressed from an admission of sin and contrition in the first week to a study of the life and death of Christ in the second and third weeks. At each stage the individual examined his own experience, read about Loyola's and compared them to those of Christ. Finally, having studied the Resurrection, the student was ready to make the commitment to become a Jesuit. The strength of the *Exercises* lay in their flexibility; individuals could progress at their own pace according to their own circumstances, and fast-track students could complete the course in ten days! Unlike Protestant faiths, these guide-lines were grounded on self-justification and individual conscience rather than on doctrine, so it was feasible for Protestants to undertake them, and many did.

What set the Jesuits apart from their contemporaries was their distinctive training and privileges. Educated for at least ten years in theology, philosophy, reasoning, logic and humanism, they combined classical with modern learning. As John O'Malley has pointed out, the Jesuits were 'the first religious order in the Catholic Church to undertake formal education as a major ministry'.[3] Steeped in self-denial and charitable experience and pledged to serve God, only the very best novices completed their training. Less than a third of these were judged suitable to take a fourth vow of obedience to the papacy. If the excellence of their education was even admired by their enemies, their privileged status was resented by most Catholics since the papacy released them from restrictive practices like fasting, wearing a clerical habit, living in an enclosed community and keeping daily choral hours, so that nothing should impede their work as ministers of the Church. In 1545 they were even exempted from episcopal control and allowed to administer sacraments, which caused further resentment. Jesuits, of course, were subject to the rules of their own order but even here they were permitted a high degree of flexibility to adapt to particular circumstances and so develop their own 'way of proceeding'.

b) The Jesuits' Work and Achievement by 1600

The Jesuits served the Catholic Church as preachers, confessors, teachers and missionaries but their most significant work in the sixteenth century lay in education and the propagation of the faith. The first colleges or seminaries were established in the 1540s to train the sons of wealthy benefactors in Italy, Spain and Portugal. They provided high quality teaching of both skills and knowledge and admitted boys from all social backgrounds free of charge. Most of the students went on to become missionaries although only a minority became priests. By 1556 there were some 33 colleges mainly in Italy, and over 230 by the end of the century. Many colleges were attached to university faculties of theology, as at Ingolstadt and Munich in Bavaria; some came to staff the entire department, as at Mainz and Würzburg in Germany, and a minority actually ran the university, as in Bamberg and Paderborn. The value of education as a means of winning over two generations – the young and their parents – was not lost on Loyola, even though it was not his intention to use teaching as a means of restoring Christian ideals when he founded the order. But he learned quickly from experience. When asked by Peter Canisius in 1554 how the Jesuits could best serve Germany, Loyola replied 'colleges'. Two years later, a college was established in Ingolstadt and Canisius became Germany's first provincial head, a post he held for 41 years. In the course of the 1560s, he became the pope's envoy in

Germany, set up 18 schools and appointed leading Jesuits to faculties of theology. In 1555 there were some 50 Jesuits serving in Germany; 20 years later, the number had risen to 400 and by 1600 there were 155 schools.

Many of the Jesuits who went to Germany were trained at a college in Rome, and similar colleges were later set up to produce English, Greek and Hungarian missionaries. Their aim was to counter the Protestant advances and, to achieve this, they played upon doctrinal differences by stressing the importance of good works, masses for the dead, confession and belief in the Virgin Mary. Loyola was contrasted with Luther: the former defended the faith; the latter, it was claimed, was intent upon destroying it. Teams of Jesuits usually targeted a community and ran a programme of events that included preaching, teaching catechisms, hearing confessions and establishing Marian Congregations. These hopefully would sustain the Christian fellowship once the Jesuits had moved on to another village. Some Jesuits blazed a well-documented trail. Jerónimo Nadal, for example, established hospitals in Sicily and tended to plague victims in Perugia (1553), Rome (1566) and Lisbon (1569). A Portuguese missionary, Francis Xavier, worked among the poor in Bologna before travelling to east Africa, Goa in India, the Malay Archipelago and finally Japan in 1551. Spanish Jesuits travelled as far as Mexico, Peru and the Philippines, and an Italian, Matteo Ricci, ventured to China. Wherever they went, thousands of natives were converted to Christianity – 10,000 in India, 200,000 in Japan, and an astonishing 650,000 in the Philippines by 1600. Faced with native opposition, for example Buddhists in China and Hindus in India, Jesuits were trained to deal with adversity. Several suffered martyrdom – 40 French Jesuits on their way to Brazil in 1570 were thrown into the Bay of Biscay by Calvinist pirates and drowned, 26 Portuguese were crucified in Japan in 1597, and in England 98 missionaries were executed for alleged treasonable activities in Elizabeth's reign – but the Jesuits remained undaunted. Their achievements were second to none in propagating and defending the Catholic faith.

3 The Council of Trent (1545–63)

KEY ISSUES What were its aims? Why were its decrees so significant to the success of the Catholic Reformation?

a) The Council's Aims

The traditional method of resolving theological and heretical problems was for the papacy to convene a general council of cardinals, bishops and abbots, and await its verdict. As we have seen, however, the conciliar movement of the early fifteenth century had threatened papal supremacy and made later popes very nervous about calling another council. In spite of the need to reform clerical and administrative abuses and to clarify theological doctrine in the wake of Lutheranism, no progress had been made. Several states, notably England, Sweden, Denmark, Norway, much of Switzerland and most of Germany, had ceased to be Roman Catholic and the threat of Calvinism was on the horizon. When a council finally met at Trent in 1545, few would have argued with bishop Bertrano's observation that 'if it will not help those already lost to the Church, it will at least help those still in danger of becoming lost'. Paul III recognised the risks involved in calling a council: his own authority could be called into question and discussion of church abuses was bound to ruffle some clerical feathers. But these were difficult times, and at least he knew that by convening the assembly in Trent, there was always likely to be a majority of Italian delegates in attendance.

Charles V's main aim was to resolve the religious schism that divided his realm in Germany and threatened his political dominance. He believed that a compromise with the Lutherans could still be achieved if only he could get them to attend, but this would not be easy. One ploy was to insist that clerical abuses were discussed ahead of doctrine. The latter was always likely to be a stumbling block but the papacy would only concede that doctrine and abuses would be discussed as alternate items, and the first session would begin with doctrine. In fact, Lutheran representatives only attended the 1552 session and, although they were cordially treated, it was clear that the majority of Catholics were not interested in reconciliation. Nor were most Lutherans for that matter. Protestantism had progressed too far, its roots were too firmly embedded. Once the German diet of Augsburg legally acknowledged the Lutheran Confession in 1555, Catholics at Trent, especially the Spanish and Italian, felt even more justified in distancing themselves from the Protestant heretics.

Suspicion that the council would be influenced more by political than religious considerations was a view held by many non-Italians. French delegates, for example, only attended the final meeting in 1562–3 when they realised they needed papal support to combat the rising tide of Calvinism. They were unable, however, to re-open any of the matters already debated at earlier sessions and were consistently outvoted by their Italian counterparts. German and Hungarian representatives were also unhappy when their attempt to authorise the celebration of communion in bread and wine was rejected, and Spanish delegates failed to carry their proposition that the pope was really the bishop of Rome and not God's representative on earth. Even when French and Spanish cardinals united to insist that bishops must reside in their diocese, the Italians demurred until a compromise solution was found. From beginning to end, nothing was decreed that did not have the assent of the papacy and Italian officials. Yet, in spite of this bias and the long duration of the council –

its 25 sessions spanned 18 years (1545–9, 1551–2, 1562–3) – the Tridentine (Latin for Trent) decrees proved to be a watershed in the history of the Catholic Church.

b) The Tridentine Decrees

What was decided at Trent? Firstly, the Catholic doctrine was clearly defined and all thoughts of a compromise with Protestantism dismissed. In fact some 33 chapters (decisions) condemned Protestant beliefs. The seven sacraments were to be treated equally; transubstantiation was confirmed as the only interpretation of the Eucharist and the mass was declared a sacrificial act, celebrated in bread only and sung in Latin. The Augustinian theology of salvation was rejected in favour of the Thomist view (due to the Jesuit presence at the council) that free will was pronounced inseparable from justification by faith. Unwritten 'traditions', which Luther had dismissed, were declared of equal authority as the written Scriptures, and the Vulgate (Jerome's Latin edition of the Bible) was declared to be free from dogmatic error although it was conceded that some textual amendments were required. Finally, belief in purgatory, indulgences, saints, images and pilgrimages were all endorsed. It was as if the Protestant Reformation had never happened.

Clerical abuses were also addressed. Discussions about how best to educate the clergy concluded that seminaries should be set up in every diocese to create an ecclesiastical ministry, that the parish clergy should preach on Sundays and feast days and be assisted by the regular clergy under the supervision of a bishop. Priests had to wear a 'becoming clerical dress, conformable to their order and dignity', and were told to keep away from taverns, plays, gambling and other sources of temptation. Marriage was not permitted for priests and clergy, and all enforced and bigamous marriages were declared unlawful but 'secret' marriages between young consenting lay adolescents were allowed. A bishop had to be legitimate, 'of mature age, and endowed with gravity of conduct and skill in letters', resident in his parish (although papal dispensations could be requested), and hold no other benefice or office. Finally, bishops were required to preach, administer the sacraments and conduct frequent synods and visitations.

c) The Significance of Trent

One of the most important results concerned the authority of the pope. Although the relationship between the papacy and bishops was not discussed at the council, every decree was submitted for papal approval. As a result, papal authority not only emerged unscathed, it was by inference supreme. Thereafter, the pope had the sole right to interpret the decrees. Laid to rest was the ghost of medieval general councils; the next one would meet in 1870. Trent was also significant because it re-affirmed the sacred authority of the clergy. Relations between priests and laymen were to be discreet and the cleric was to distance himself from the laity in terms of his dress, social conduct and celibacy and so emphasise his distinctive role as the intermediary between commoners and God. All men were not priests in the eyes of the Catholic Church. The vital role of the bishop was also apparent. Abuses had been identified and remedies approved; it now fell to the bishops to effect the reforms. This was particularly true in their overseeing of pastoral and teaching duties, and the establishment of seminaries. Some historians regard these training colleges as one of the council's most important legacies. In the opinion of Hubert Jedin, 'if the Council of Trent had done nothing else for the renewal of the Church but initiate the setting up of diocesan seminaries for priests, it would have done a great deal'.[4] In the long run, this is true but the period before 1600 saw few established: 20 in Spain, 11 in Italy, a handful in Germany all of which closed down or were taken over by universities, and none in France. Limited financial and human resources proved a more serious obstacle than the Tridentine fathers had imagined.

To many contemporaries and later historians the real importance of Trent lay in its refusal to compromise traditional doctrinal beliefs. Its decrees embodied 'Rome's defiant riposte to the challenge which the Protestant reformers had thrown down'.[5] Not only did it meet the challenge by agreeing upon a definition of its theology – something which Protestant theologians had singularly failed to achieve – it showed that it was willing to adapt to the needs of the people. By condoning saints, relics and pilgrimages and the efficacy of good works, the Church was able to build upon local and popular customs and so rescue them from the attacks of Protestant reformers. Admittedly, the difference between sacred and profane rituals, between superstition and piety, was often blurred but the Catholic faith maintained its medieval appeal to millions of uneducated and God-fearing people. Thus pilgrimages to Santiago and Montserrat retained their popularity in Spain; Italian lepers still bathed in the sea on Easter Saturday; and a host of benedictions to protect humans, animals and inanimate objects from misfortune was incorporated into the Catholic liturgy. Protestants continued to condemn such beliefs but the Catholic Church saw the advantages of accommodating them until their followers were educated in the true faith. In this respect, the Church had little option once it rejected Luther's denunciation of superstitious practices.

Though Trent restructured the Church's administration to meet the challenges ahead and so became more relevant to the people, it was notably silent on several important matters. Little was said about the future role of the regular orders beyond their requirement to be monitored by bishops, and the new orders, Inquisition and Index received even less attention. As far as women were concerned, they were only discussed at the final session when it was decreed that all female orders must be cloistered and brought under monastic rules. The decrees were also silent about the curia. The question of its reform had been on the agenda but decisions had been skilfully deferred due to the sensitivity of the issue. Twenty years later the papacy would finally attempt to put its own administration in order (see page 103).

The achievements of Trent were considerable. Ironically, when it finally ended in December 1563 it did so not because it had completed all of its business – the Breviary (prayers), Missal (rites governing the celebration of the mass) and Catechism (an elementary textbook for priests) had still to be authorised – but because it was feared Pope Pius IV was about to die. His promulgation of the decrees and canons in June 1564 was the high-water mark of his pontificate and a turning-point in Catholic history.

4 Repression of Heresy

> **KEY ISSUES** How did the Catholic Church deal with heresy? Was it successful?

a) The Inquisition

Protestant writers have tended to attach an exaggerated importance to the Inquisition in respect of the sixteenth-century Catholic Reformation. The Spanish Inquisition had operated continuously since 1480 and though at first used to investigate *conversos* (Jews who had been converted to Christianity), by the 1520s its tribunals were targeting Erasmians, *alumbrados* (mystics and illuminists) and Lutherans. Few were found and only at the start of Philip II's reign did it become particularly active against heretics. Between 1559 and 1562, some 278 heretics were prosecuted and 77 put to death. Thereafter, the courts were more concerned with lapsed *conversos*, *moriscos* (Muslims who had converted to Christianity) and allegations of blasphemous and immoral behaviour. Nevertheless, there were marked regional variations: the inquisitors in Barcelona, Saragossa and Seville, for instance, heard more cases of heresy than most other tribunals but after 1562 Protestantism was never a serious problem in Spain. The threat of arrest and the stigma attached to being a suspect proved a powerful deterrent. Although fewer than two per cent of those arrested were actually burned at the stake, the acquitted carried a burden of shame which was shared by their family too. Moreover no one was above suspicion, as bishop Carranza, the primate of Spain, discovered. Arrested on a charge of heresy in 1559, he spent 17 years in Spanish and Italian prisons before being released without a trial or conviction.

Between 1523 and 1566 over 800 executions occurred in the Netherlands. Charles V had first issued placards (published ordinances) against Luther in 1522 and appointed two inquisitors to enforce them. As auxiliaries to the Dutch bishops, these inquisitors were given increasing authority to suppress heretics, and Anabaptists and Lutherans were their chief victims. Philip II expanded the practice in 1561 to combat Calvinism: 14 new bishops were appointed each assisted by two inquisitors. These changes were instrumental in bringing the Dutch to revolt. Philip's response was to impose martial law and treat the insurgents as rebels not heretics: the Council of Troubles subsequently arrested 12,000 suspects and sentenced 1,100 to death. France, like the Netherlands, never had a permanent inquisition in the sixteenth century. Instead it relied on the secular law courts and *parlements* to suppress heresy. In 1525 the Paris *parlement* campaigned against suspected Lutherans and supported the death penalty for anyone who read, translated or printed heterodox material. The accession of Henry II in 1547 saw the *Chambre Ardente* created to try heresy cases and ten years later an edict imposed the death penalty on anyone found preaching without a licence. The growth of Calvinism in France in the second half of the century, however, was not suppressed by the courts, and the Church was powerless to prevent a lengthy religious civil war (see page 119).

Both Portugal and Rome established permanent inquisitions during this period. Portugal had few problems of heresy in 1547 when a tribunal began in Lisbon but a concern over purity of blood and the presence of many *conversos* troubled Catholic consciences. The Roman Inquisition on the other hand was much more active. After the failure of the Regensburg colloquy and the defection to Lutheranism of Bernardo Ochino and Peter Martyr, both high profile Catholic reformers, Paul III feared heresy was about to spread throughout northern and central Italy. An Inquisition was therefore established in Rome in 1542 and regional tribunals set up in Milan, Lucca, Florence, Venice and Naples. Like its Spanish counterpart, the Roman Inquisition was successful in removing pockets of Protestantism and by the 1580s was actually more concerned with cases of immorality and witchcraft. In fact more than 50 per cent of cases heard between 1560 and 1614 involved offences connected with personal pleasure – like dancing on Sundays and boisterous behaviour during holy festivals.

b) The Index

Much of the Inquisition's time was spent in authorising the publication of books and licensing literature. Indices were first issued by universities to censor their students' reading as early as 1479 and in the 1520s it was the Sorbonne in Paris and Louvain university in the Netherlands which first outlawed Luther's writings. The Sorbonne went on to publish 25 articles defining heresy in 1543 and four years later was permitted to censor all religious works in France. Louvain produced its edition of forbidden books in 1546. Elsewhere, city authorities such as Siena (1548), Venice (1549) and Milan (1554), responded to local pressure and produced their own list of prohibited reading.

The first Roman Index of 1559 proscribed over 500 authors. Among them, in addition to the leading Protestant writers, were Boccaccio, Rabelais, Machiavelli, some 50 vernacular Bibles and 14 works by Erasmus. Five years later, a more select list known as the Tridentine Index was published, although Erasmus was still bracketed with Luther and Calvin. Unlike other Catholic states, Spain did not acknowledge the Roman Index and so the inquisitor-general, Valdés, compiled his own in 1559. Some 670 works of mainly foreign origin were condemned though regional tribunals had their own variations. In 1583 the Spanish Index was expanded to include 2,375 titles and for the first time incorporated titles which had been expurgated (offending passages were excised). It is hard to gauge whether these indices effectively shielded Catholics from allegedly harmful material. Though the volume of Protestant literature entering Catholic countries remained small, forbidden works still circulated sometimes due to undetected false titles but often the result of smuggling. More effective censorship was probably operated by the universities. As already noted, theological faculties controlled by Jesuits (as at Ingolstadt) or by Dominicans (at Cologne) were more successful at promulgating Catholic ideas in the long term than were any state directives.

c) Mass Appeal

A more positive method of countering Protestant ideas and spreading Catholic beliefs was the printing press (see page 129). By simplifying its faith in catechisms, prints, paintings, plays and songs, and by producing a vast amount of devotional material, the Church instructed its congregations and tried to wean them away from their attachment to popular beliefs. Catechisms were particularly important in offering a basic instruction in obedience and in expounding prayers, the Creed and the Ten Commandments. The confessional also provided a perfect opportunity to re-inforce Catholic virtues and correct personal vices. These private and, for some Catholics, regular meetings between priest and penitent contrasted with the occasional and highly public confessions of the medieval Church.

The significance of visual culture especially painting should not be understated. The Council of Trent insisted that all art must be free of false doctrine and accurately depict church history. Nudity was declared indecent and the human body as portrayed by Renaissance artists was condemned as profane. Paolo Veronese, for instance, had to explain to the Venetian Inquisition why several fictitious figures appeared in his version of the Last Supper. The Church indicated what kind of art it wanted when the Accademia di San Luca opened in Rome in 1577, and five years later cardinal Paleotti wrote a treatise outlining what was acceptable to Catholic censors. Thus, Tintoretto's 'Last Supper' (1592), which shows Christ in a circle of light passing the host to an apostle while servants carry on with their menial tasks, was warmly received. Such works of art were just as eloquent and in some respects more effective than the printed word in spreading the message of the reformed Catholic Church.

5 Spiritual and Secular Reformers: the Reformation in Italy and Spain

> **KEY ISSUES** How important was the papacy in leading the Catholic renewal? What was the significance of cardinal Borromeo? How far did the Church in Spain experience a reformation under Philip II?

a) Catholic Reformation Popes

Most of the popes between 1555 and 1600 played a key role in advancing the Catholic Reformation and improving the condition of the Church in Italy. Several were saintly men who lived austerely; and all were Italian. Paul IV (1555–9) established the Index and gave his backing to the Inquisition, which he had begun in 1542, to root out heretics in Italy. In many respects the Catholic Reformation marked time during the pontificate of this outspoken opponent of Spain, the Jesuits and general councils. His successor Pius IV (1559–65) seemed like a throwback to the pre-Reformation era – he fathered three children and practised nepotism – but by re-opening the Council of Trent and seeing its work through to completion, he performed a great service. Much was also achieved under Pius V (1565–72). Reforms to the Catechism, Breviary and Missal were completed and he went some way towards enforcing the decree on episcopal residence in Italy. Personally ascetic, he visited the poor, tended to lepers in hospital and expelled prostitutes from Rome. Gregory XIII (1572–85) continued in the same vein. For two years he planned for the jubilee celebrations of 1575, aware that thousands of pilgrims would visit his city. Derelict sites were cleared and new buildings commissioned. He also encouraged Jesuits from the Roman college to conduct missions to England, France, Poland and Germany. Indeed it was due to Gregory that papal nuncios were first sent to Switzerland, Austria and Germany to supervise the Tridentine decrees. The Wittelsbachs, a staunch Catholic family from Bavaria, received his backing to ensure their client became the prince-bishop of Cologne in 1583 and archduke Albert was allowed to tax the Bavarian clergy and control many ecclesiastical offices in return for publishing the decrees.

Reform of the papal curia was long overdue but took place during Sixtus V's rule (1585–90). 15 congregations or departments of state were set up to administer papal affairs. Six dealt with temporal business, such as the navy and the university, and nine were concerned with spiritual matters, like the Inquisition and the Tridentine decrees. In addition, Sixtus continued to rebuild Rome: a new library was opened, statues of saints were placed on top of ancient columns, and in 1590 St Peter's cathedral had a new dome. The next three popes – Urban VII, Gregory XIV and Innocent IX – lasted less than two years between them but Clement VIII (1592–1605) had a more lasting impact. He revised the Vulgate (1592), issued a new Index (1596) and ordered a general visitation in Rome. In 1600 some three million pilgrims attended the jubilee celebrations in a city which had undergone a remarkable transformation in recent years. Michael Mullett is right in claiming that the period between 1563 and 1600 was 'critical to the rebuilding of the institution's [i.e. the papacy's] power and prestige in early modern Europe'.[6]

b) The Work of the Italian Clergy

Where the papacy led, Italian cardinals and bishops followed. The Catholic Reformation had as much to do with individuals as institutions, a fact well illustrated in Italy in the second half of the sixteenth century. The peninsula was not politically united so churches could be reformed at the behest of individual bishops and city councils. Some reformers were no doubt inspired by a tradition of civic humanism but many were caught up in the spiritual zeal to improve the lives of their community. Giberti had already shown what could be achieved in Verona (see page 90), and the north and central Italian bishoprics in particular saw several dedicated men such as Feltre della Rovere, archbishop of Rimini (1565–78), Gabriele Paleotti, archbishop of Bologna (1566–97), and Carlo Borromeo, archbishop of Milan (1565–84). These bishops implemented the Tridentine decrees, resided in their dioceses, founded seminaries and conducted regular visitations. Borromeo, who presided over the largest archdiocese in Italy, set a standard that was hard to follow. He convened six provincial councils and 11 synods, established three seminaries and over 700 schools, set up a printing press, regularly discussed problems with his clergy, and gave away much of his own money to help plague victims in Milan in 1576. It is not surprising to find that Borromeo's reputation survived him and in 1610 he became a saint.

A different picture emerged to the south of Rome where the dioceses were small, frequently impoverished and understaffed. In the kingdom of Naples, for instance, where the Inquisition had no jurisdiction and strong family ties saw few advantages in clerical reform, abuses such as simony, non-residence and concubinage persisted. Here the social work of lay charities, confraternities and Jesuits proved more valuable than the creation of seminaries or holding provincial synods. It was the spiritual and social needs of these deprived people which inspired Philip Neri, a Jesuit, to establish the Congregation of the Oratory in 1575 in Rome and Naples, an order which would spread to Catholic communities throughout the world. These men worked amongst the poor, preaching, teaching and administering the sacraments.

c) The Spanish Church under Philip II, 1556–98

Outwardly Spain seemed to be a strong, united, Catholic country, largely unaffected by the Protestant heresies in northern Europe. As we have seen, the Inquisition was effective in stifling Protestantism and suppressing dissident ideas. Yet all was not well in the Church in Spain and when he acceded to the throne Philip, a most ardent Catholic, was determined to implement root and branch reforms. Many lower clergy were uneducated and impoverished; pluralism and absenteeism were rife; and the spiritual development of the laity appeared to have been arrested. As a consequence, many people's faith still lay rooted in pagan rituals and superstitious practices. Ignorance of Christianity not interest in Protestantism was the problem. The upper clergy were far from blameless. The highest offices remained the preserve of the nobility, many of whom were non-resident, and there was constant friction between monastic orders, bishops and inquisitors.

Philip waited until the Tridentine decrees were published and, in 1564, put them into operation. Six provincial synods met in the following year and 20 seminaries set up in the course of his reign. 12 Franciscan convents were founded in La Mancha, 17 monasteries in Madrid and 80 Discalced Carmelite houses throughout Spain. The latter was a new order for women begun by Teresa of Ávila in 1562, that was committed to a life of contemplative prayer and social work. Jesuits were also very active. Pedro de León, for example, worked all over Andalucia and Extremadura, setting up missions in these remote provinces. Spanish priests were ordered to preach a weekly sermon, use the Roman Missal and Breviary in their services, give religious instruction and start Sunday schools. The confessional became a very important means of instructing the laity and, for their part, congregations were expected to attend weekly masses, take communion at Easter, and live a moral and virtuous life.

Were these good intentions translated into deeds? Was this new spirit of Catholicism more than a seven-day wonder? The evidence is hard to interpret and at best inconclusive. What seems likely is that the impact of the Catholic Reformation varied according to the personal drive of the bishops, the contribution of Jesuits and the interest and cooperation of the laity. Cardinal Quiroga, archbishop of Toledo (1577–94), worked closely with the king, held numerous synods and saw the level of Christian understanding in his dicoese rise. At Philip's accession, only 37 per cent of people questioned by the Toledo Inquisition could recite their prayers; in the 1590s, nearly 70 per cent could. In Valencia, archbishop Juan de Ribera began a financial scheme to raise his priests' stipends, founded a seminary and a college to educate *moriscos*, and for 43 years devoted himself to the reformation of the Church.

In contrast, there was plenty of evidence supplied by inquisitors and missionaries that many areas of Spain remained spiritually backward and indifferent. In 1572 one inquisitor noted that Galicia, in the north, had 'no priest or lettered persons or impressive churches or people who are used to going to mass and hearing sermons ... They are superstitious and the benefices so poor that as a result there are not enough clergy'.[7] Similar stories of peasant ignorance and clerical inadequacy existed elsewhere. It seems that communities remained closely attached to their local cults, carnivals and fiestas, and were unwilling to change. The continuing veneration of unauthorised images in parish churches was the subject of synods held at Granada in 1573 and Pamplona in 1591 where the Inquisition bemoaned the low level of Christianity.

6 Conclusion

'Counter or Catholic Reformation?' For a number of years historians have debated this question. Until the 1970s, it was a commonly held view that the Catholic Church introduced reforms as a direct consequence of the Protestant Reformation. 'After the unexpected shock of the Reformation', wrote Harold Evennett, 'the old church underwent a spiritual revival and an administrative renovation.'[8] It was generally claimed that until the 1530s a corrupt papacy lived in fear of a general church council, and that the Catholic revival evident in the second half of the century owed a great deal to Luther and very little to medieval precedents. Since the 1970s, historians have revised this view of the Counter-Reformation. Although some scholars, like Geoffrey Dickens and Nicholas Davidson, continued to use the term, they were increasingly aware of the fifteenth-century origins of the Catholic revival. Indeed most if not all of the principal features of the Catholic Reformation had medieval precedents: orders dedicated to charitable work, general councils, reform-minded popes, the Inquisition, individual piety, mysticism, and so on. Certainly it is now fully acknowledged that the Church learned much from the Protestants – how to promote its cause, how to be more relevant to the people, and how to avoid doctrinal disputes, for example. Certainly the Protestant Reformation provided the context for Catholic reform and, to some historians, it was a catalyst too. Nevertheless as long as the term 'reformation' is used, it is likely to imply that Protestants played a significant part in shaping the history of the Catholic Church, a suggestion that is resented by some Catholic historians. Whether a more acceptable phrase will be coined to describe the sixteenth-century Catholic reform movements remains to be seen. R. Po-Chia Hsia has suggested 'Catholic renewal' and Robert Bireley prefers 'Early Modern Catholicism'. For the moment, the phrase 'Catholic Reformation' seems an altogether more accurate description and is favoured by most modern historians.

Where and why was the Catholic Reformation successful by 1600? We have seen how Italy and Spain lay at the heart of the galvanised Catholic Church, how Jesuits, missionaries and lay orders took Christianity to the people, and how secular and spiritual leaders effected improvements once the Council of Trent had completed its work. If success is measured in the number of Protestant states returning to the fold, then it was successful. Poland, Austria and Hungary had been in danger of going Calvinist but remained Catholic, and the Lutheran territories of Swabia, Franconia, the Rhineland, Carinthia, Styria and Bohemia reverted to Catholicism. In each case, a combination of secular powers and missionary activity proved an effective formula. Indeed, the greatest success was to the south and south-east of the Holy Roman Empire where Capuchins and Jesuits worked alongside the Austrian Habsburgs and Wittelsbach dukes to enforce the Tridentine decrees. By 1600 an arc of cities from Munich in the south-west to Salzburg, Linz, Vienna and Prague in the south-east held the Catholic line. In addition, the majority of France and the Netherlands stayed Catholic in spite of a strong Calvinist presence, and only a handful of German princes became Protestant in the second half of the sixteenth century.

Did the spiritual condition of these Catholic communities actually improve? The extant evidence suggests that the spiritual development would be a long and slow process. Much depended on the education and commitment of the clergy if abuses were to be minimised and the quality of preaching and religious instruction improved. Only Spain and Italy had established enough seminaries by 1600 to see some tangible improvements; simony, absenteeism and nepotism remained at all levels of the Church, and the nobility continued to control patronage of the highest offices. Portugal and Spain fared better than Germany and France. In fact, few reforms were introduced into France before the 1620s and Paris did not have a seminary until the 1690s. It is a salutary reminder that the Catholic Reformation was a diverse and patchy affair, which owed more to its teachers and preachers than to institutional reforms in Rome. Borromeo, Neri, Teresa and Canisius were the real inspiration behind the Church's new vitality. Communities clung to their religious traditions and only by adapting the official teachings to these localised conditions would the

Church regenerate their spirituality. It was to be a long process that would continue well into the eighteenth century.

Footnotes

1. J. C. Olin, *Catholic Reform: From Cardinal Ximenes to the Council of Trent, 1495–1563* (New York, Fordham U. P., 1990), p. 57.
2. *The Constitutions of the Society of Jesus*, trans. G. E. Ganss (St Louis, 1970), pp. 66–7.
3. J. W. O'Malley, *The First Jesuits* (Harvard U. P., Camb., Mass., 1993), p. 15.
4. H. Jedin, *Crisis and Closure of the Council of Trent: A Retrospective View from the Second Vatican Council*, trans. N.D. Smith (Sheed and Ward, 1967), p.120.
5. B. M. G. Reardon, *Religious Thought in the Reformation* (Longman, 1995), p. 284.
6. M. Mullett, *The Catholic Reformation* (Routledge, 1999), p. 111.
7. H. Kamen, *The Spanish Inquisition* (Phoenix, 1998), pp. 255–6.
8. H. O. Evennett, 'The Counter-Reformation' in J. Hurstfield (ed), *The Reformation Crisis* (Arnold, 1965), p. 58.

Answering synoptic questions on Chapter 6

Synoptic questions seek to draw together different aspects of the History course which you have been studying and are an integral part of the A2 specification. They test your understanding of historical continuity and change over one hundred years or more to see if you can explain key moments and turning-points. In the case of the Catholic Reformation in the sixteenth century, you need to develop a broad overview of the period and show appropriate links and comparisons with related topics. Factual details are certainly important but should be used only to demonstrate and support your understanding of historical perspectives relevant to the question. Consider the following questions:

1. Was the Counter-Reformation during the sixteenth century anything more than a reaction to the Reformation?
2. 'Without the co-operation of rulers, the Catholic Reformation could not have succeeded.' How accurate do you consider this opinion to be?
3. How far did the influence of the papacy change during the sixteenth century?

Let us examine Question 1. Most students will suggest that the Counter-Reformation was much more than a response to the Protestant Reformation, and the highest marks are likely to go to responses which link the nature and characteristics of the Catholic movement to the pre-Reformation as well as to the Protestant period. Ensure that you distinguish between the terms 'Catholic' and 'Counter-Reformation'. The Council of Trent, for instance, was occasioned by the Protestant challenge and many of its decrees emphasised their theological differences but Trent was much more than a knee-jerk reaction to Lutheranism. So too were the lay and spiritual orders, especially the Jesuits. Their origins lay in the socially deprived towns and villages of Italy and Spain, not the heretical lands of Germany and Switzerland. You should stress that the Catholic Reformation was principally concerned with improving the quality of the clergy and making their spiritual and pastoral work more relevant to the prevailing moral and social conditions. As a result, Catholic missionaries, preachers and teachers had a lot in common with their Protestant counterparts. While many Jesuits came to see themselves (and were seen) as agents at 'war' with heresy, their contribution to the Catholic Reformation was much wider. The role of church leaders should also figure in your answer. If the papacy before and after the pontificate of Paul III offers a nice contrast in change, the work of bishops Viterbo, Giberti and Borromeo demonstrates a continuity of ideas and dedication which will earn you good marks.

Summary Diagram
'The Catholic Reformation'

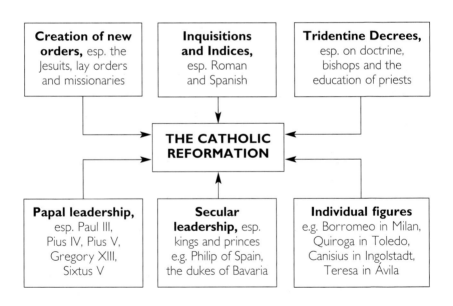

7 The Effects of the Reformation

POINTS TO CONSIDER

The Reformation had far-reaching effects which left no corner of Europe and no section of society untouched. This chapter considers its impact thematically upon religious, political, economic, social and cultural affairs during the sixteenth century.

KEY DATES

1522	Imperial knights' war in Germany.
1524–6	German peasants' revolt.
1530	Augsburg Confession.
1531	Formation of the Schmalkaldic League; end of civil war in Switzerland.
1536	Pilgrimage of Grace rebellion.
1546	Schmalkaldic war between Charles V and Lutheran alliance.
1547	Battle of Mühlberg.
1549	Zurich Consensus (Consensus Tigurinus) drafted by Bullinger and Calvin; Prayer Book rebellion in England.
1552–5	Second Schmalkaldic war; Peace of Augsburg (1555).
1559	Scottish rebellion of the Lords of the Congregation.
1562	Massacre of Vassy begins the French Wars of Religion.
1569	Revolt of the Northern Earls in England.
1572	Outbreak of the Dutch Revolt; Massacre of St Bartholomew's Day.
1577	Formula of Concord.
1598	Edict of Nantes ends the French Wars of Religion.

1 Religious Impact of the Reformation

> **KEY ISSUES** What was the confessional composition of Europe in 1600? Why was there so much confessional violence? What was the spiritual condition of the clergy and laity?

a) The Age of Confessionalism

In the course of the sixteenth century, the Christian Church in western Europe was split into a variety of confessional faiths. This was not an inevitable development. Indeed, in the early years following Luther's excommunication, most Catholic and Protestant leaders met to heal the schism, but without success. We have already seen that in Germany in 1530 Charles V received the Augsburg Confession drawn up by Luther and Melanchthon and a variation of it from four south German cities presented by Bucer (see page 42). Both proposals were rejected by orthodox theologians whose uncompromising attitude proved a serious obstacle to reconciliation. Nevertheless Charles persisted in trying to find a peaceful solution. Further conferences were held at Hagenau, Wörms and Regensburg but, just when an agreement seemed possible, Luther and the pope raised fresh objections. By the mid-1540s, Charles' patience was wearing thin, the first session of a general council of the Church had been called and Germany was divided into two confessional faiths – Lutheran and Catholic – a condition which was confirmed at Augsburg in 1555.

Between 1545 and 1563 the Council of Trent produced a series of decrees based on traditional beliefs which did much to demonstrate Catholic strength and unity. The mainstream reform movements, on the other hand, were far from united. A meeting at Marburg (1529) had confirmed the gulf between Luther and Zwingli. In 1536 the leading Swiss cantons established their own Helvetic Confession, which later became the United Swiss Reformed Church. Although neither Berne nor Basle joined and the central cantons remained staunchly Catholic, the Second Helvetic Confession of 1566 confirmed that confessional peace was attainable – at least in Switzerland.

The emergence of Calvinism made unity of faith within Protestant Europe even less likely. Calvin's ideas raised fundamental questions about the first generation of confessional beliefs: were they indeed appropriate for the next generation of reformers in the face of a resurgent Catholic Church? Could Protestants present a more united front? The 1550s saw Luther's successor, Melanchthon, attempt to reach a compromise with Bucer and Calvin, but little was accomplished. Instead a rift had developed in the Lutheran camp between Melanchthon, who was always willing to make concessions to Catholics, and more militant-minded Protestants, who questioned the direction that German Lutheranism was taking. Their differences were finally resolved in 1577 by the Formula of Concord which defined the Lutheran doctrine and rejected any compromise with Calvinists. By this time, however, untold damage had been done to the image of German Lutheranism and only a handful of towns had taken it up since Augsburg.

The majority of Protestants in Germany were Lutheran but the future of European Protestantism lay with Calvinism. Of the 28 German principalities which had become Calvinist by 1600, the Palatinate was by far the most important. Its Heidelberg Confession was the creed used by most German reformed churches and, outside Germany, Calvinism proved more attractive than Lutheranism, establishing itself in Hungary, Poland and Transylvania in eastern Europe, and in Scotland, France and the Netherlands in the west. In England, the Elizabethan Church faced two serious challenges: firstly, the arrival of Catholic missionaries and Jesuit priests encouraged recusants to defy the religious settlement of 1559; secondly, discontented Protestants agitated for the Genevan Prayer Book and a small number of presbyterians separated from the Church of England. By 1600 many leading bishops, including the archbishop of Canterbury, were expressing Calvinist ideas but the queen defended her Church resolutely.

Europe, then, was a confessionally divided continent in 1600 (see the map on page 112). Most of the north was Protestant: Scandinavia was Lutheran, as was most of northern and central Germany; the northern Dutch provinces held some 10 per cent Calvinists but Anabaptists lived there as well; England and Scotland were solidly Protestant, as was much of Switzerland; and between 5 and 10 per cent of France was Huguenot. In contrast, Portugal, Spain and its dependencies, most of France and Italy, and much of southern Germany, remained Catholic. A combination of traditional cultures, autocratic rulers, missionary activity and the shadow of the Inquisition, had left little room for Protestant sects. Eastern Europe was the most confessionally mixed area due principally to the large territorial principalities, the constant threat of the Turks and the political patronage of many nobles. In Bohemia, for instance, a confession based on the ideas of Lutherans, Hussites and the Swiss Brethren was produced in 1575, and Calvinism and Catholicism were also widely practised. In neighbouring Moravia, the radical Hutterites were protected by local nobles and in Poland, Unitarians (who rejected the Christian view of the Trinity) co-existed with Catholics, Lutherans and Calvinists.

b) Religious Violence and Persecution

Confessional differences brought acts of violence unprecedented in the history of Christianity. 'We attack images but Catholics attack people', was a widely held Calvinist view. Indeed church images and the followers of reformed and counter-reformed faiths were the targets of sectarian persecution. Why was this? From the outset, Protestants regarded relics, shrines and religious images as contrary to the second commandment – 'Thou shalt not worship graven images' – and set out to destroy them. Though Luther disapproved of iconoclasm, both Zwingli and Calvin encouraged the lawful removal of graven images. From time to time violence did break out when passions were roused and town authorities held back from exercising restraint. Wittenberg, for instance, experienced several months of violence in 1521–22; Catholic magistrates in Basle resigned in protest in 1529 at the lack of action against iconoclasts; many English churches and monasteries were looted in 1538; and France witnessed endemic disturbances between 1555 and 1562. Some of the worst violence occurred in the Netherlands in 1566 when Calvinists in seven towns ransacked Catholic churches and convents in five days of riot-

112 The Effects of the Reformation

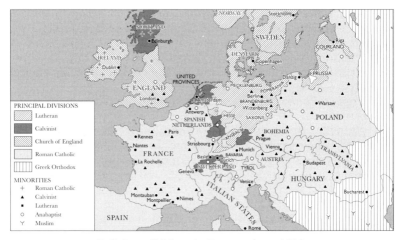

Religious divisions in Europe about 1600.

ing. The numbers of people involved varied from town to town and their motives were not exclusively confessional but the impact on Catholic officials and neutral observers was one of general fear and private anger.

Not surprisingly, popular violence bred acts of retaliation, sometimes connived at and sometimes authorised by magistrates. Certainly where political authority was weak and Catholic feeling strong, an undercurrent of sectarian reaction was always capable of destroying the veil of peaceful co-existence. In the eyes of many Catholics, Protestants were the Devil's agents and had to be destroyed. In France, entire communities took oaths to defend their faith and to hunt down Huguenots as if they were wild animals. In 1562 massacres occurred at Vassy, Sens, Tours, Angers and Carcassonne and, at Bar-sur-Seine, 140 Protestants were murdered by Catholic soldiers in August alone. By far the worst atrocities took place in August and September 1572 when in excess of 30,000 Huguenots were murdered in cold blood. It would, however, be inaccurate to suggest that French Protestants were incapable of retaliation: news of local murders and personal losses undoubtedly hardened confessional attitudes. Huguenots in the Midi, for example, swore 'never [to] trust those who have so often and so treacherously broken faith and the public peace; never [to] disarm as long as the enemy continues to oppose the true faith and those who profess it; and [to] sign no peace treaties that can be used to start massacres'.[1]

In fact, Protestants had a well-documented history of religious bigotry and intolerance towards each other, as well as against Catholics. Luther and Zwingli consistently condemned radical sects, Calvin persecuted anyone who deviated from his canon of faith (see page 60), and Beza described liberty of conscience as a 'thoroughly diabolical dogma'. Catholic writers held similar views. Thomas More had always believed that heresy bred disorder, and a Spanish Jesuit, Juan de Mariana, argued that 'the day that gives freedom of worship puts an end to the happiness of the Commonwealth'.[2] Most governments persecuted heretics. Laws had long been in place and methods of enforcement ready to deal with divergent beliefs. The Spanish Inquisition turned its attention from investigating *moriscos* and *conversos* to targeting foreign merchants, sailors and visiting workers suspected of Protestant heresy; in the Netherlands, Alva executed over 1,100 heretics between 1568 and 1573; and, in England, 283 Protestants went to their death in Mary's reign and more than 220 Roman Catholics were executed or died in prison in Elizabeth's reign.

c) The Condition of the Clergy

Few groups suffered more than the clergy as a result of the Reformation. They were swept along by the winds of change and scattered according to the political and religious dictates of their masters. Whenever a ruler or town council contemplated ecclesiastical reform, clerical groups found their lives turned upside down. Should a priest defy the pope and centuries of orthodoxy and run with the reformed church or should he resist change, forego his livelihood and perhaps put his life at risk? Some clergy turned Protestant, took the opportunity to get married and accommodated themselves to change; some resisted the Reformation for as long as possible either passively or actively; and some caried on regardless, protected by their patron and supported by their parishioners.

The regular clergy were most affected by the Protestant Reformation. Chantries and monasteries closed down, monks and nuns were pensioned off, and many found themselves unemployed and homeless. A minority of male clergy re-entered ecclesiastical life but most probably sought work in their community, while most nuns appear to have returned to their families. Protestant pastors and ministers found themselves in demand but salaries remained low and their responsibilities increased. Now ministers were expected to preach as well as teach, and this required an improvement in the general level of education. The quality appears to have varied regionally and nationally. In England, there was a shortage of preachers for much of the century: only one quarter of Oxfordshire parishes in 1586 had regular sermons, and in Peterborough in 1576 only 40 out of 230 ministers could preach. Some towns such as Coventry and Leicester established lectureships to pay for visiting preachers and Calvinist bishops, like Parkhurst and Grindal, encouraged Bible classes known as prophesyings to raise the level of preaching. The situation was little better on the continent. One quarter of churches in Calvinist Béarn in France in 1598 were without well-qualified ministers and even Geneva experienced a serious shortage of men entering its university to become pastors. Regular visitations conducted by secular authorities now identified such shortcomings and generally recorded an increase in graduates holding benefices in Protestant churches, but there were still complaints that many parishes were too large for pastors to fulfil their work effectively.

The Catholic Church had also tried to improve the condition of its clergy but most states only implemented reforms after Trent in the second half of the sixteenth century. Progress was therefore slow and patchy. The establishment of seminaries would have a major impact on the quality of priests but by 1600 their effect had been variable. Portugal had introduced seven and Spain 20, but France had none until the seventeenth century. In Germany, few criticisms were raised in the diocese of Würzburg but there were anti-clerical complaints in Trier and Cologne where concubinage was still a problem. Similar criticisms were voiced in Spain. Salaries were generally low and pluralism remained widespread; absenteeism was a particular problem among Aragonese bishops. Not until the eighteenth century would several German and Austrian parishes experience the full effects of the Tridentine decrees.

Complementing the parish priests were the regular and new Catholic orders, and these underwent significant changes as a result of the Reformation. The Dominicans, for instance, exercised an increasing influence upon the papacy, Inquisition and Index, and the Benedictines saw an increase in its members. The Capuchins (reformed Franciscans) actively promoted Catholic preaching, teaching and charity work and the Jesuits contributed substantially to improving the quality of Catholic clergy. Generally, the Catholic Church was in a far stronger condition in 1600 than in 1500. Its institutions had been reformed, its headship confirmed and the relationship between the pope and his college of cardinals, and between bishops and parish priests, more clearly defined. There was still much to be done but the structure was in place for further progress.

d) The Spiritual Condition of the Laity

We have already suggested that there was a steady improvement in the quality of clerical teaching and preaching, and we could reasonably expect the laity in Catholic and Protestant countries to have developed a better understanding of Christianity. Was this indeed the case? The picture which emerges is far from clear partly because historians have failed to agree upon how to define religious commitment. For instance, how much doctrine did a person have to understand before he/she could be regarded as 'reformed'? Secondly, since reformers constantly strove to achieve perfection, they consistently fell short of their ideals and often wrote in correspondingly depressed terms. Eamonn Duffy reminds us that 'the rhetoric of reform is not so much a measure of the failure of that project [the achievement of a Christian society], but of the vitality of their commitment to it'.[3] We must therefore guard against accepting at face value the complaints and criticisms of poor lay standards of spirituality yet still take them into account in our assessment. This is far from easy.

The evidence for Catholic states suggests that people were reluctant to forego their links with traditonal customs and remained deeply attached to devotional aids of penitence. Saints, pilgrimages, holy relics and religious ceremonies held a magnetic appeal which the Church could neither break nor afford to ignore. Superstition, witchcraft and the efficacy of good works often overlapped, and it was frequently reported that most Catholics had little understanding of Christian theology. Nevertheless, the Spanish Inquisition reported improvements in Cuenca, where 80 per cent of those examined in the 1570s could recite their prayers, and in Toledo, where a decade later, some 70 per cent could do so.

More is known about the condition of Protestant states from the visitation records, catechisms and consistory courts in particular. The overall impression we get is one of widespread gloom. Evangelical pastors in Germany complained of uninterested congregations. In the 1570s, Lutheran Saxon visitations record children absent from catechism classes, while parishioners preferred to go fishing and drinking rather than attend services; and the Calvinist Palatinate visitations of 1593–5 recorded that many people did not know the Lord's Prayer. Similar conditions seem to have existed in France and the Netherlands. Calvinism was extremely popular among literate urban-dwellers and a crowd of 5,000 gathered near Antwerp in 1566 to hear 'hedge-priests' preach in open fields, but the general level of literacy was simply not high enough for many peasants to read or understand the reformed faith. Perhaps, as the historian R. Po-Chia Hsia suggests, this was because Calvinism was an 'abstract, intellectual religion of the élite'.[4] Ministers in England similarly claimed that few attended weekday services, only children regularly learned catechisms and most people showed little interest in theology. George Gifford suggested in 1581 that in Essex 'ye shall not find five among five score [100] which are able to understand the necessary grounds and principles of religion'; ten years later, William Perkins similarly complained that whether people went to church or prayed at home, 'there be no understanding'.

What, then, are we to make of this evidence? First, many rural areas were slow and at times unwilling converts to the Protestant faith. People remained closely attached to traditional practices and resented change. Second, the Protestant emphasis upon the Bible and its rejection of devotional aids and good works appealed to more educated groups. Since literacy levels were low and all faiths stressed the importance of catechisms in raising the laity's level of doctrinal knowledge, their audiences were likely to be limited. Finally, many found the reformed churches, both Protestant and Catholic, imposing and intruding. Few laymen attended more than one service a week, many were reluctant to learn catechisms and, although communion was available, most only received it at Easter. Quite simply, Lutheran pastors, Calvinist preachers, Puritan ministers and Catholic priests demanded more than the laity were prepared to give. Many of the former were over-zealous; most of the latter were spiritually indifferent.

2 Political Effects of the Reformation

KEY ISSUES What were the main consequences of the Reformation for secular and spiritual rulers? Why did the Reformation cause so much civil distress?

a) The Growth of Secularism

In the 80 or so years after the 'Lutheran affair', more than half of Europe had adopted some form of Protestantism. As we have seen, the desire to improve the spiritual condition of the Church and enhance people's understanding of Christianity, could be a compelling reason for adopting one of the Protestant faiths. To separate confessional from other motives, such as political or economic, may be considered unwise and even impossible, yet we should recognise that some reformations were inaugurated principally to increase the political power of secular rulers. Gustavus Vasa of Sweden and Christian III of Denmark, for instance, formed an alliance with their nobles against the Catholic bishops, issued Lutheran orders and seized church lands. Similar developments occurred in Finland, Norway and Iceland. Henry VIII was another ruler who benefited from the secularisation of church property when his revenue doubled from the acquisition of monastic lands.

The desire to achieve political independence, not so much from the Catholic Church as from the Holy Roman Emperor and ruling élites, largely explains why much of eastern Europe became Protestant. In Bohemia and Moravia, it was not the king but the nobility who decided the faith of their provinces, and many became Lutherans or remained Hussites in the course of the century. A similar situation existed in eastern Austria where the nobility and local estates embraced Lutheranism to stop the ruling Habsburgs from centralising their lands. Eastern Europe, of course, faced the additional threat of being overrun by Moslem Turks and, as central governments collapsed, lesser nobles and leading magnates took control of their churches and turned Lutheran.

It was in the Holy Roman Empire, where anti-papal sentiment was strong and the authority of the emperor less than secure, that the princely, noble and urban reformations were most clearly seen. The desire to strengthen their declining military and political power in particular explains the support given to Luther by several imperial knights. By the same token, their adversaries, the princes, seized the chance to gain church lands and discipline their subjects more effectively. Traditionally, the right to implement reform was reserved to each German prince. Frederick of the Palatinate, who became a Calvinist in the 1560s, spoke for many when he acknowledged that controlling religion was vital to his rule, 'the basis of all temporal and heavenly welfare'. In this climate of political change, the imperial cities and larger towns believed that conversion to Lutheranism, Zwinglianism or Calvinism would give them greater protection from princely interference. Nuremberg, Strasbourg and Augsburg took control of church affairs but did so cautiously, partly because they were unsure how the Catholic emperor would respond and partly to minimise the risk of popular reactions for or against reform. In Switzerland, where first Zwinglianism and later Calvinism became popular in Protestant inclined cantons, effective political control rested with the city magistrates and elected councils. The tight control exercised by local authorities over their inhabitants' lives largely explains the growth of Calvinism in countries where there was no centralised administration or where the ruler was weak.

As the authority of secular rulers increased, that of the papacy declined. This development was already under way in England, France and Spain, where kings exercised considerable control over clerical taxation and appointments, but was a novelty in Germany, Scotland and Scandinavia. The Reformation accelerated this process. In England, the sovereignty of the crown was confirmed as 'supreme' in 1534 and, in harness with parliament, denied the pope any temporal or spiritual authority. In Germany, the peace of Augsburg (1555) not only recognised the right of each prince to decide whether to be Catholic or Lutheran, it also tacitly acknowledged the limits of papal rule. As a consequence, Germans were much more likely to identify their interests with that of their state and ruler than with a foreign pope. Catholic rulers outside Germany – in Portugal, Spain, Italy and France, for instance – also took advantage of confessionalisation to extend their control over their subjects.

The most tangible examples of diminishing papal influence can be seen in taxation, patronage and the law. Instead of paying tithes, annates, dispensations and fees to the pope, payments either ceased altogether or were collected by the state. In some cases, such as Sweden and England, the crown actually received more taxation than before the Reformation. The appointment of clerics and control of ecclesiastical patronage was another source of political and financial power seized by the state. Salaries were controlled, posts filled or left vacant (to the benefit of the patron) and the right of presenting to offices eagerly sought by competing families. Finally, in every Protestant country with the notable exception of England, church courts were replaced by secular courts, canon law was supplanted by civil law, and clerical privileges ceased to exist. In England, however, church courts, canon law and various benefits enjoyed by the clergy largely continued with modifications until the nineteenth century.

b) Wars, Revolts and Political Violence

The sixteenth century was an unstable period in history: there were dynastic wars, social and economic rebellions, and political revolts in most countries, and from the 1520s onwards, a new cause of instability – the Reformation. Few states escaped the effects of religious change; each attempted to keep the lid on a boiling pot and preserve a semblance of political control. In this section we will examine a range of countries which experienced war, rebellion and civil disorder, caused principally by the Reformation.

Germany saw fighting between rival religious groups in 1522 when a small number of imperial knights took up Lutheranism to revive their flagging political fortunes. Their defeat at Landstuhl at the hands of the princes was a timely reminder where power in the Empire really lay, a fact borne out by the protection some of the princes accorded Luther and by the ferocity with which they suppressed the peasants' revolt of 1524–6. These disturbances were in part due to social and economic grievances but they were also due to the assumed belief that Luther's 'priesthood of all believers' entitled them to seize landlords' property. For two years some 100,000 peasants rebelled in much of the south and west of Germany before order was restored.

The refusal by Charles V in 1530 to allow Lutheran princes to celebrate their faith led to a large military organisation being set up at Schmalkalden and, with it, the likelihood of a confessional war. Not until 1546 was the emperor ready to challenge the Protestant princes. In spite of a resounding victory at Mühlberg, Charles soon found an alliance of Catholic and Lutheran princes ranged against him which proved decisive. The Peace of Augsburg ended the conflict in 1555 and allowed each prince to determine whether he wished to rule a Catholic or Lutheran state. There was no place for Calvinism, Zwinglianism or Anabaptism, and no reference was made to the imperial cities. Nevertheless, religious peace held in Germany for more than 60 years. The first confessional war in Switzerland in 1531 ended almost as soon as it began. Fighting between the Christian Civic Union (Zwinglians) and the Christian Alliance (Catholics) lasted a few days and resulted in a Protestant defeat and the death of Zwingli. The Swiss cantons, however, took the ground-breaking decision to respect each other's faith, and there were no further problems.

Tudor England experienced no religious wars but it did face three rebellions from discontented Catholics and a series of plots to assassinate Elizabeth I. While each of the rebellions in 1536, 1549 and 1569 had a variety of causes – political, social and economic – the Catholic reaction to reforms in the English Church was a key feature. Indeed, each rebellion had the Five Wounds of Christ as a symbol of Christian intent. In October 1536, 30,000 rebels gathered in Pontefract and called for the restoration of monasteries, papal authority and an end to Protestant heresy. The rebels were dispersed and the ringleaders hanged but Henry VIII was shaken by the scale of the protest. A smaller rebellion, confined to the south-west counties, occurred in 1549 when some 6,000 demonstrators marched to Exeter in protest against the new prayer book and called for the restoration of traditional Catholic practices. The Edwardian government was unimpressed and a royal army slaughtered the rebels at Clyst St. Mary. A desire to return England to the Catholic fold was a principal reason why some northern earls and local gentry raised their tenants in revolt in 1569. Significantly, although 5,000 protesters overran much of Durham and Yorkshire, they were not supported by northern nobles and the disturbances were slowly suppressed. Catholic plots to release Mary, Queen of Scots, from captivity occurred in 1571, 1583 and 1586, and added to the climate of political insecurity caused by religious discontent. Yet Elizabeth avoided confessional warfare mainly because she was unwilling to persecute loyal Catholics and prudently kept at bay the pro-active puritans. It was a difficult task to perform but the queen succeeded.

Scotland was the first country to establish a presbyterian church as a result of a political uprising. Patriotic Scots resented the rule of the Catholic French court in Edinburgh which from 1558 threatened the freedom of Protestant landowners and caused the 'Lords of the Congregation' to start a rebellion. Their resulting success in 1560 was due in no small way to the rallying-cry and organisation of John Knox, a Calvinist preacher recently returned from Geneva. In practice, the lowlands and major towns became Protestant but the highlands and north-eastern isles remained Catholic, and tension between presbyterians (who wished to abolish bishops) and episcopalians (who wanted to retain them) was never far away.

The two countries which saw most violence in the sixteenth century were France and the Spanish Netherlands. Each lacked a government strong enough to suppress a determined Calvinist minority, each had Catholic armies which were superior in size but unable to achieve victory, and each saw sectarian killings on an unprecedented scale. Perhaps as many as 50 per cent of the French nobility were drawn to Calvinism in the years between 1555 and 1562 and conservative estimates suggest that at least one million people were attending 2,000 Protestant churches. A powerful Catholic king might have succeeded in stemming this heretical tide but a succession of weak monarchs from

1559 opened the way for rival French families, each with its own agenda, to seek to defend the faith by violence. For nearly 40 years, France experienced brief periods of warfare punctuated by short spells of reconciliation. Permanent peace was only likely when the monarch was strong enough to keep rival factions apart, when most people accepted that too much blood had been shed and when Huguenots and Catholics realised that neither of them could win. In 1598 a compromise settlement was arbitrated at Nantes by Henry IV. The Catholic faith remained the national religion but Huguenots were permitted equal civil liberties, military security and religious freedom in 100 designated towns.

Most of the 17 provinces of the Spanish Netherlands experienced continuous fighting from 1572 until 1579. Thereafter the seven northern provinces continued their struggle against Spanish rule until independence was finally achieved nearly 70 years later. The Dutch Revolt was not just about religion – there were constitutional, political, economic and social factors at work too – but the confessional divide between Spanish Catholicism and Dutch Calvinism was too great to bridge. As in France, neither faith was strong enough to suppress the other. The Calvinists were always a minority and unwilling to countenance religious or political compromise but it was their determination and self-belief which helped fortify them in their revolt.

In contrast to the west European states, most countries in eastern Europe saw little sectarian violence and no wars in the sixteenth century. However, when the demands of Calvinists and Lutherans increased and the influence of Jesuits on Catholic rulers began to take effect towards the end of the century, violence erupted – in Hungary in 1604, Poland in 1606 and Bohemia in 1618. Wars of religion were most certainly not confined to the sixteenth century.

c) Obedience and Resistance

A major consequence of the Protestant Reformation was the idea that subjects could resist their ruler if he was denying them freedom of religion. It had long been held that rulers had a Christian duty to govern justly and, in return, subjects were expected to be obedient. From the 1520s onwards, important questions had been raised: who held power in the state, the emperor, princes or people? Was armed rebellion ever justified? In 1525 an anonymous German peasant pamphlet, *To the Assembly of Common Peasantry*, had justified resistance against tyrannical lords and cited biblical precedents in fighting for 'godly law'. Unsurprisingly, those in authority, and the leading Protestant theologians, disagreed. Nevertheless, theories of resistance continued to be developed among Protestant lawyers and they acquired the support of German princes and cities as Lutherans sought to justify their disobedience to the emperor. He was elected by the people, it was claimed, and if he denied them the true faith, then they had the right to defend themselves.

This political theory was first applied by the Lutheran princes in 1546 and proclaimed by the city of Magdeburg in its *Confession* of 1550. By then Calvin was also beginning to re-think his position. At first, in 1536, he had condemned popular disobedience arguing that 'if anything in a public ordinance requires amendment, they [the people] should not raise a tumult or try to correct it themselves, but should commend the matter to the judgement of the magistrates'.[5] But who were the magistrates? They were those in authority, appointed by the people, declared Calvin, but they could only rebel passively. This equivocal stance was unsatisfactory to English, French and Dutch Protestants in the 1550s, when confronted with acts of Catholic repression. John Knox, the Scottish presbyterian, justified opposition to Mary's Catholic Reformation on the grounds that she had broken her contract with God and His people, and they were entitled to resist this ungodly ruler. An English writer, Christopher Goodman, went even further in his work, *How Superior Powers Ought to be Obeyed* (1556). Kings were accountable to the people, he claimed, and lesser magistrates (nobles and justices) could act in the name of the people. If they failed, the people must act on their behalf. Calvin would not go this far but he did respond to pressure from French Huguenots in the early 1560s and condoned resistance by princes of the blood against Catholic repression.

Some French Protestants, however, were prepared to go further and in the 1570s developed their own theories of resistance. In Beza's *The Right of Magistrates* (1574), lesser magistrates were obliged 'to offer resistance to flagrant tyranny', and du Plessis Mornay in his *Defence of Liberty against Tyrants* (1579) claimed that 'the Church was committed and entrusted to the people as a whole' and 'God wished to have the people intervene'. While French Catholic apologists, such as Jean Bodin, stood firmly against this concept of popular sovereignty, others began to express arguments in favour of tyrannicide in the 1580s when a Huguenot claimant to the throne seemed likely. Indeed, the murders of William of Orange (1584) and Henry III (1589) by fanatical Catholics may have owed something to this ambivalent relationship between subject and ruler. The Reformation had strengthened the power of the state but it also raised questions about the status of the ruler. Some would use the Church in the future to make the state more absolute; others would work with the Church to impose limitations on the monarchy.

3 Economic Effects

> **KEY ISSUE** How did the Reformation affect finances, commerce and levels of employment?

a) Financial Issues

The economic advantages enjoyed by secular rulers when they took control of their churches was one of the main attractions of becoming a Protestant. Money from the sale of ecclesiastical property lined the pockets of German princes in the 1530s, and the Swedish and Danish kings, who secularised monastic lands, did so to replenish crown revenue and build up political support. Catholic as well as Lutheran rulers profited. Henry VIII first acquired and then disposed of monastic lands, plate and jewels, to provide the treasury with more than £1,000,000 and the seizure of chantry lands under Edward VI provided a further £25,000 a year in rent. Episcopal lands were also taken and, although some bishops received increased tithes and rectories, most incumbents saw a sharp fall in their overall revenues.

The economic condition of the Church was more affected on the continent. In towns, cities and states where Protestant reforms had occurred, church property was commandeered and salaries, which were generally low, were paid by the state. Tithes and offerings continued to be paid by the laity in both reformed and traditional churches and, although rebellious peasants in Germany, Denmark and England had complained about paying tithes, Lutherans, Zwinglians and Catholics like Henry VIII all argued that tithes were a customary and legal practice, and the law must be obeyed. In effect, those in authority wished to maximise their revenues and not loosen the economic bonds which constrained the peasantry.

b) Commerce and Trade

In A. G. Dickens' celebrated phrase, the Reformation was 'an urban event'. There is little doubt that the commerce and trade of merchants, artisans and craftsmen were particularly affected. Apart from the considerable expansion in printing and engraving, which accompanied the publication of religious tracts and polemical propaganda, new business opportunities opened up. Protestant cities were well ahead of their Catholic rivals in both the volume and range of publications. Existing trade links were also strengthened along confessional lines – Swabian and Rhenish towns traded with Zurich, Basle and Schaffhausen, London traded with Hamburg, and Amsterdam with Emden – but businesses could be adversely affected too. South German and Swiss towns that might have turned Lutheran or Zwinglian could not afford to anger their Catholic Habsburg and Bavarian nieghbours and, as a result, chose to compromise their religious reform programme rather than risk losing valuable trade.

Religious differences produced thousands of refugees, as groups of displaced people migrated in search of a more tolerant society. The resulting economic impact on a town or region could be significant. In the 1520s Duke Albert of Prussia, for example, encouraged Dutch Anabaptists to settle to help his state's economy recover from recent wars with Poland, and Moravian nobles saw the advantages of inviting persecuted Mennonites to work on their lands. Gustavus Vasa in the 1530s encouraged Dutch refugees recently exiled from Denmark to settle in Sweden and develop their tapestry and goldsmith skills and, later in his reign, Bohemian Brethren and Dutch craftsmen were invited too. In German Augsburg, a policy of bi-confessionalism was practised and advocated by two influential Catholic merchant families, the Welsers and Fuggers, who were keen to promote wealth for themselves and their city.

Perhaps the country whose commercial prosperity was most adversely affected by the Reformation was the Netherlands. Charles V had persecuted large numbers of Anabaptists but held back from encroaching upon the commercial privileges enjoyed by many Dutch Lutherans. He needed their tax contributions and profits from trade as much as the town authorities and understood the reason why towns such as Groningen and Antwerp refused to enforce heresy edicts. Philip II, however, was less tolerant and his repressive religious and political measures led to some 100,000 Protestants leaving the Netherlands between 1567 and 1590. Antwerp, its main commercial city, suffered most. It was occupied by foreign troops and many of its leading bankers emigrated to Frankfurt, London and Amsterdam.

For much of the twentieth century economic historians were attracted by the views of Max Weber, who claimed that certain features of Protestantism appealed to the hardworking, thrifty, capitalist merchants and town-dwellers. The elect, he argued, could identify themselves by their commercial initiative, enterprise and subsequent wealth, and Beza's justification for usury (interest charged on loans) served to underline this early form of capitalism. Today, historians no longer accept Weber's thesis. They have found it simplistic, impossible to verify and, in certain cases, untrue. Luther and Calvin did not believe that material success and individual faith should be bracketed. Calvin saw communal not individual providence to be the results of God's blessing and, though it was acceptable to charge interest to cover possible commercial losses, neither reformer totally approved of usury. Of course, in practice not all Calvinists were merchants, craftsmen and proto-capitalists and not all successful businessmen were Calvinists but, at its most basic level, Protestantism was an altogether less expensive faith than Catholicism and no doubt some Calvinists did believe that God helped those who helped themselves.

c) Employment

A little considered consequence of the Reformation was the diminishing opportunities for work and the many clerics who found themselves unemployed or unemployable. Exact numbers affected by the dissolution of monasteries and chantries are impossible to calculate – the surviving evidence is neither accurate nor complete – but as monasteries, convents and hospitals closed down or were converted to secular uses, thousands of men and women, many of them elderly, were forced to live off their pensions, return to their families or seek local employment. While a minority of male clerics remained in the Church, some converted to the reformed faith or looked for work in schools, almshouses and infirmaries. Women were hit the hardest. Not only were their pensions quite small, nuns could not continue to work in the secular church and the opportunities to work as cooks, nurses and domestic servants would not necessarily have appealed to them. Moreover, Protestant communities sought to close brothels and charitable institutions, both of which had offered sources of employment for women.

4 Social Effects

> **KEY ISSUES** In what ways were standards of behaviour and social customs affected by the Reformation? How did the Reformation influence the relationship between rich and poor, and between men and women in society?

a) Standards of Behaviour and Social Customs

The Reformation ushered in much more than religious, political and economic change: it inaugurated important social consequences too. In the early 1520s the first generation of Protestant reformers saw the need to establish and maintain levels of behaviour and social conduct in keeping with their godly reformation. This desire to uphold public morality was in part a result of the disorderly behaviour which both Luther and Zwingli had witnessed, and in part it was due to their belief that they had a moral duty to establish guidelines for the good of the community and the continuation of the reform movements. As a consequence, both Calvinist and Catholic states were to impose strict rules governing standards of behaviour.

'Without discipline there could be no church', declared the radical leader Menno Simons. While no theologian would have argued with this view, two questions arose: how could discipline be enforced and how intrusive would the state and Church become? In every Protestant country except England, moral standards were regulated by secular authorities through consistory courts. In England, although the canon laws were reformed and made subject to the common law, the church courts continued under episcopal control, and dealt with all cases of matrimonial, moral and sexual concern. Catholic states sought to impose discipline through the church courts, administered by bishops and through inquisitions in Spanish and Italian lands, but also attached considerable importance to confessionals as a direct way of correcting abuses and upholding discipline. In both reformed and traditional churches, the threat of exclusion from communion was the principal deterrent against anti-social behaviour while every effort was made to help people resolve personal problems. Preserving communal unity was more important than excluding people from society.

Calvin set out his moral code in a *Book of Discipline*. Gambling, swearing, drunkenness, dancing in public were all condemned, as were women who dressed outrageously or were given to wearing excessive hair styles. Thus Madame du Plessis-Mornay was excluded from communion in Calvinist Montauban on account of her bouffon hair and Francesca Perrin was banned from Geneva because she enjoyed dancing. Attempts to enforce this reformation of manners were not always successful, and visitation records suggest that miscreants were not easily discouraged. Laws prohibiting pre-marital sex, for instance, seem to have been ineffective in spite of the recognised dangers of sexually transmitted diseases. Though most Protestant and Catholic authorities closed municipal brothels, prostitution continued to be practised either clandestinely or outside city walls. Some Italian cities, such as Florence and Venice, regulated the activities of prostitutes and funded asylums for girls and women at risk. Such reforms had begun before the Reformation and developed apace in the course of the sixteenth century.

Perhaps inevitably, a number of traditional practices were subjected to reform. Both Protestants and Catholics wanted to end pagan and unchristian activities in order to achieve greater social control. Festivals, such as Carnival, May Day and Candlemas, were enjoyable occasions and, in spite of attempts to remove them from the church calendar, continued in many Protestant states. While the celebration of saints' days and medieval customs, like ringing bells on All Hallows, were discouraged and gradually discontinued in many Protestant countries, these and many more traditional customs continued in Catholic states. Belief in the devotional power of prayer to appease souls in purgatory was underlined at Trent, and chantries went from strength to strength in the post-Reformation era. The Catholic Church recognised the need to enhance popular folklore and to channel local practices towards mainstream Christian beliefs.

The attitude of the Catholic Church towards magic and witchcraft is a case in point. Condemned by Protestants as superstitious and by the papacy as deviant, witchcraft was nonetheless widely practised both before and after the Reformation. White witches were considered harmless and were regularly consulted to alleviate personal problems; black witches, on the other hand, were harmful and practised 'maleficia'. Magic and religion clearly overlapped. People's fear of black witches may well have increased when the Protestant churches rejected intercessory prayers and no longer offered protection through spells and exorcisms. Certainly in the course of the sixteenth century, and especially after 1560, witch-hunting increased. Some historians, like Hugh Trevor-Roper, have attributed this to 'the social consequence of renewed ideological war and the accompanying climate of fear'.[6] Confessional conflicts often accompanied the persecution as rival sects accused each other of consorting with the Devil, and both Protestant and Catholic communities targeted dissenting groups. Between 1560 and 1600, many areas of Germany, France and Switzerland saw an increase in persecutions, but it should be noted that several Catholic and Protestant countries, such as England, Scandinavia, Spain and Italy, saw few if any cases of witch-hunting. Clearly non-religious factors were also at work. Political leaders, for instance, saw witches as heretics and persecuted them as a demonstration of their piety and power. Some authorities targeted spinsters and widows because, like Jews and gypsies, they were minority groups and easy scapegoats for unexplained misfortunes. There was a significant correlation between the incidence of witch-hunting and local economic crises, and, if state authorities failed to take prompt action, villagers often resorted to violence. It seems probable, then, that the number of persecutions rose when years of religious and political instability coincided with periods of rapid economic and social change.

b) Social Relations: Rich and Poor

It was not the intention of Protestant reformers to change the relationship between rich and poor. In Calvin's opinion, there had always been poor people and it was God's intention that there always would be. Nevertheless, the Reformation did force all authorities to confront the problem of rising numbers of beggars and to distinguish between those who were genuinely incapable of work and those who were too idle. The first generation of reformers saw the need to make provision for the poor; in the case of Lutherans and Zwinglians to minimise the likelihood of civil disorder and, in the case of Anabaptists, to fulfil the prophecy that the meek should inherit the earth. Indeed many of the German miners, weavers and peasants who revolted against their landlords in 1524 believed that the Reformation would bring them equality and freedom. They called for a reduction in their lords' social and economic power and a halt to their attempts to re-introduce feudalism, as well as the abolition of serfdom and the death penalty. The defeat of the peasants, however, confirmed the established social order and indicated that Protestantism would primarily benefit the ruling classes. Thus, in Germany, Scandinavia and England, the territorial princes secured control of ecclesiastical patronage, thereby depriving many nobles of their traditional livelihood. In Austria, France, Bohemia and Hungary, it was the nobility who gained control.

One of the most important social reforms was the permanent provision for the urban poor. All Protestant theologians and several Catholic writers had joined humanists in condemning the monastic and mendicant orders: they called upon people to give charitably to hospitals and the poor rather than buy indulgences or found chantries. Luther and Zwingli, and Catholic humanists like Erasmus and Vives, held the view that individuals had a Christian duty to help one another; social welfare was the natural extension of spiritual welfare. Luther called upon every town to ban begging and Wittenberg and Nuremberg were among the first in 1522 to provide work for the unemployed and help for the sick, old and infirm. In the following year he developed his ideas in the Leisnig Order by recommending that communal donations should be put into a common chest to pay for public works and houses for the poor. Leisnig became the model for towns and villages throughout Lutheran Germany and there is little doubt that Luther's ideas had a profound impact. In the opinion of Robert Jütte, 'the discussion of Luther's principles of relief and their effects in the sixteenth century shaped the centralised poor relief system not only in early modern Germany but also elsewhere in Europe'.[7]

Bucer and Calvin took a more structured approach towards poor relief and appointed deacons to supervise its collection and distribution. In England poor boxes appeared in churches in the 1530s and several town corporations acquired former monastic hospitals and almshouses. One result of this municipal initiative was the increase in private contributions: after 1540, private charity, much of it from merchants, was ten times greater than local poor collections and often endowments were accompanied by explicit instructions from the donor. In 1587, for instance, David Smith founded six almshouses in London for widows on condition that 'they shall be no swearers nor blasphemers of the name of God, nor no drunkards nor scolds, nor disquieters of other people'. Similar developments occurred in Catholic states. Begging was condemned and, following the lead by Juan Vives in Bruges in 1526, poor houses were enclosed and regulated to establish permanent well run institutions. The mendicants continued to help the poor and Jesuits and other secular orders worked with them but, whereas before the Reformation charitable bequests had been in decline, now they too were increasing.

c) Men, Women and the Family

The Reformation was essentially a male movement. All theologians and church leaders were men and almost all preachers. Women were expected to be silent, obedient and chaste. Although some women played a part as wives of reformers, worked for lay charities or became mystics in the Catholic movement, the Reformation re-affirmed the fifteenth-century values of a patriarchal society. That said, several important changes did take place in the relationship between men and women.

One of the most significant developments concerned marriage. In rejecting its sacramental nature, Protestants introduced several reforms. First, the clergy was free to marry and many did. Luther believed that marriage was a natural condition and the genesis of the family; the values which governed the family provided the foundations of a godly society. Second, the state controlled marriage and the laws determining the age of consent. The canonical age of 12 for women and 14 for men was raised in many areas to 20 and 24 respectively, in an attempt to give parents greater control over their children. Anyone who married without consent could be disinherited. Third, arranged marriages became illegal – which was a major step towards liberalising young girls as well as young men. Fourth, divorce and re-marriage were made possible but discouraged. In fact, magistrates primarily considered the economic effects on individuals and the community and only occasionally granted requests. Consistory courts tried hard to reconcile couples rather than impose sentences or transfer cases to magistrates, and the voluntary act of separation, which had happened in the past, was frowned upon in an attempt to save a marriage. Marriage and divorce now required careful consideration: marriage was a public act of personal commitment; divorce was a private act against the best interests of the community. In contrast Catholics accused reformers of desacrilising marriage and undermining moral values by making divorce easier. Re-marriages were declared illegal as were clandestine marriages – those without parental consent or between under-age partners – unless conducted by a priest in front of witnesses. Indeed medieval services had not always been conducted by a clergyman or in a church but, after the Reformation, services had to be held in a church by a minister or priest, who solemnised the union by kissing the ring as a symbol of peace and friendship. Marriage had therefore been transformed 'from a social process which the Church guaranteed, to an ecclesiastical process which it administered' and divorce was only possible with papal dispensation, and specifically for adultery, abuse or heresy.[8]

In both Protestant and Catholic states, male heads of households acquired more control over the religious and moral welfare of their family. Women had their place in society, which was confirmed by nature, the law and the Bible, and that was to be subordinate to men. Yet it was important, argued Luther, that men shared the housework, looked after the children, and upheld the standards of behaviour in the household. The Catholic Church similarly stressed the husband's authority within the family. A wife had a duty to obey her husband but he had a responsibility to treat her with care and affection. In practice, gender roles were defined more strictly as a result of the Reformation: the husband was the bread winner who commanded the workplace and was head of the family; his wife was largely excluded from the work force, was politically disenfranchised (she could neither vote nor hold public office), and was unable to hold land except through inheritance, run a business or company, and was excluded from university. Her main role was to get married. Indeed, unmarried women were held up for criticism and prostitutes condemned.

Historians are in serious disagreement as to whether the condition of women in the sixteenth century improved as a result of the

Reformation. Luther did much to dispel two traditional beliefs: that women's prime function was to have children and that, as sexually insatiable creatures, they presented a danger to men and society. In his view, 'men cannot do without women'. Certainly, as a result of Protestant reforms, women received equal rights concerning adultery and divorce, and under-age girls could not in theory be exploited by under-age or arranged marriages. These were positive achievements in an overwhelmingly patriarchal society. Yet male prejudices remained. Calvin believed that the idea of women governing men was 'utterly at variance with the legitimate order of nature', a view held by freedom-loving Anabaptists as well as by conservative-minded Jesuits. The ideal woman read the Bible, married, instructed her children and obeyed her husband. And if a man changed his faith, his wife was expected to conform.

5 Culture

> **KEY ISSUES** What impact did the Reformation have on literacy and education? How were developments in painting, sculpture, architecture, music and drama affected by the Reformation?

a) Literacy and Printing

Although historians generally agree that perhaps 30 per cent of town inhabitants could read but less than ten per cent of all people were literate, they disagree as to the role of literacy in spreading the Reformation. Certainly while pamphlets were cheap, books remained expensive throughout the sixteenth century. Luther acknowledged the importance of the word as a means of spreading the Gospel but he fully understood that low literacy levels meant children and simple folk would be 'more easily moved by pictures and images to recall divine history than through mere words or doctrines'.[9] Luther's German Bible of 1534 accordingly had 118 illustrations. As the desire to understand the Bible and acquire copies of sermons, devotional works and catechisms increased, so the Reformation helped to spread literacy, but it was the printing presss which truly revolutionised this process.

All reformers agreed that printing made vernacular studies possible and brought to each person who could read the power to think and reason independently of the Church. 'God's highest and most extreme act of grace' was Luther's judgement on the printing press, and the seven presses that operated in Wittenberg helped to make him a cult figure throughout Germany. The Reformation soon became a vehicle for confessional propaganda as rival faiths sought to increase their following. The Lutheran engraver Georg Pencz, for example, in *The Content of Two Sermons,* contrasted Protestants steeped in Bible studies with Catholics playing with their rosaries. Catholic apologists responded in like kind but their propaganda was generally less extensive and effective. If printing did not cause the Reformation, it definitely helped to promote reform; and the Reformation in turn demonstrated for the first time the power of the press.

b) Education: Schools, Colleges and Universities

Both Protestants and Catholics saw education as a principal instrument in advancing the Reformation: society needed educated people to provide teachers, preachers and state officials, and the community had a moral duty to provide good schools. Luther regarded the secularisation of monastic and cathedral schools as a good opportunity to regulate elementary, secondary and higher education. His church orders standardised teaching in villages and towns through the use of catechisms. These simple question-and-answer texts were used to teach children and adults how to memorise and understand basic doctrinal beliefs. Calvin also put great store in regular testing of catechisms both in the home and in church and hundreds of catechisms were printed during this period. Catholics recognised their merit too and unashamedly adapted Protestant editions. The German Jesuit Peter Canisius, for example, copied Luther's catechism and Emond Auger adapted Calvin's for use in France. It was the Jesuits, in particular, who saw the advantage of continuous education and established colleges for 10 to 22 year-olds that produced students capable of becoming future church leaders and teachers. Before long, there was a massive expansion in university education. Many Catholic-controlled universities, especially in Germany and Italy, came to be run by Jesuits but Calvinist foundations, like Heidelberg and Herborn, were equal to them in respect of their teaching and publications.

c) Painting, Sculpture and Architecture

The visual arts were among the first victims of the Protestant Reformation. The Second Commandment encouraged reformers to smash statues, deface paintings and defile church ornaments and, although Luther discouraged iconoclasm, he was powerless to prevent the destruction of many works of art. In Switzerland, only images in stained glass windows survived the reformers' hammer, since they were widely admired by Zwinglians and Catholics alike, but Calvinists wanted to remove these as well to produce churches that were plain and relatively colourless.

Woodcuts, engravings and paintings were used by first generation reformers as a means of propagandising religion. Luther believed that works of art should be free from icons and preferred paintings of the Passion of Christ, the Last Supper and the Resurrection, and Calvin discouraged religious themes altogether. As a result, portraits, landscapes and domestic scenes became popular with many Dutch and French Protestant painters. The Catholic Church on the other hand took a more positive view of painting, frescoes and sculpture. Trent had decreed that 'all lasciviousness must be avoided so that figures shall not be painted or adorned with a beauty inciting to lust'.[10] Instead, art was to inspire and instruct the observer. The saints, the Virgin and the crucifixion thus became acceptable and popular subjects for Spanish and Italian artists.

Church architecture also underwent major changes during this period. Side chapels and rood lofts were dismantled, stone altars were replaced with wooden tables, and the chancel enlarged so that ministers could be seen and heard more easily. Catholic churches also became wider and more spacious. The Jesuit church in Rome, Il Gesu, begun in 1568, with its massive façade and large interior, and the Theatine church of S.Andre della Valle begun in 1591, with its large nave and flat roof, characterised this new style of baroque architecture.

d) Music and Drama

Most Protestant reformers had a high regard for music. Luther placed it second only to the Word of God, and composed hymns, metrical psalms and vernacular polyphonic chorales. Muntzer and Bucer composed hymns and 50 of Calvin's psalms were set to music. By 1600 more than 4,000 Protestant hymns and songbooks of motets had been published. Only Zwingli of the early reformers had a total dislike of music; it had no biblical or theological justification and, in his opinion, detracted from the church service. The Catholic Church was restrained in its musical taste. Trent had decreed that 'all things should be so ordered that the masses, whether they be celebrated with or without singing, may serenely reach into the ears and hearts of those who hear them, when everything is executed clearly and at the right speed'. The tempo therefore was slow and syllables were articulated clearly. Plainsong and polyphony became fashionable and were successfully combined in the works of Palestrina, the choirmaster of St Peter's in 1551.

Drama fared even better in the hands of Catholics. Jesuits used plays as a religious medium to inform and instruct, and religious conversions, saints' lives and biblical scenes were popular themes. Open-air performances sometimes attracted thousands of spectators and were an effective way of propagating the Catholic message. Protestants, on the other hand, downgraded drama and regarded religion as generally unsuitable subject matter. In England mystery and miracle plays were no longer being performed by the end of Elizabeth's reign and, on the continent, any play with a religious theme had to reflect the 'true faith'. Significantly, plays about Luther were being written in Germany and contributed in no small way to the development of his cult-worship. He would have been appalled.

Footnotes

1. Cited in R. Knecht, *The French Wars of Religion* (Longman, 1989), p. 109.
2. G. Lewy, *Constitutionalism and Statecraft during the Golden Age of Spain* (Geneva, 1960), p. 90.
3. E. Duffy, 'The Long Reformation: Catholics, Protestants and the multitude' in N. Tyacke (ed), *England's Long Reformation, 1500–1800* (University College of London Press, 1998), p. 37.
4. R. Po-Chia Hsia, *Social Discipline in the Reformation: Central Europe* (Routledge, 1989), p. 154.
5. J. T. McNeill (ed), *Institutes of the Christian Religion* (London, 1960), p. 151.
6. H. Trevor-Roper, 'The European Witch-Craze of the Sixteenth and Seventeenth Centuries' in *Religion, the Reformation and Social Change* (Macmillan, 1977), p. 140.
7. R. Jütte, *Poverty and Deviance in Early Modern Europe* (CUP, 1994), p. 108.
8. J. Bossy, *Christianity in the West, 1400–1700* (OUP, 1985), p. 25.
9. Luther's *Passional* (1522).
10. H. J. Schroeder, *Canons and Decrees of the Council of Trent* (TAN Books, Illinois, 1978), p. 217.

Essay questions on Chapter 7

This chapter has considered some of the main effects of the Reformation. In answering the following questions, you should not only re-read the relevant sections of this chapter but also consult other sections in this book, as well as additional articles and reading material. Remember that it is very unlikely that one book will provide you with a complete answer to these or to any other A Level History questions.

1. Why was there so much confessional violence in sixteenth-century Europe?
2. In what ways and why did secular rulers benefit from the Reformation?
3. What were the main effects of the Reformation on European economies?
4. How much did the Reformation change the role and importance of women in society?
5. How far were cultural developments affected by the Reformation in sixteenth-century Europe?

Summary Diagram
'The Effects of the Reformation'

POLITICS	**RELIGION**	**ECONOMICS**
Secularism	Confessionalism	Finances
Papacy	Violence	Commerce
Warfare	Clergy	and trade
Resistance	Laity	Employment

THE EFFECTS OF THE REFORMATION

SOCIETY	**CULTURE**
Customs	Literacy
Rich and poor	Education
Men, women	Fine Arts
and the family	Performing Arts

Further Reading

General textbooks

M. Greengrass, *The European Reformation*, (Longman Addison Wesley, 1997) is an easy-to-consult reference work containing a mine of factual information; and **E. Cameron**, *The European Reformation* (OUP, 1991) provides an excellent introduction to the doctrinal beliefs and theological developments of this period. **G. Elton**, *Reformation Europe* (Blackwell, rev. ed., 1999) adds little to his classic account, first published in 1963, and his *The Reformation* (New Cambridge Modern History, vol. ii, CUP, 1990) contains a series of excellent articles. **C. Harper-Bill**, *The Pre-Reformation Church in England 1400–1530* (Longman, 1989) offers a succinct and well-devised assessment of the English Church. **A. G. Dickens**, *The English Reformation* (Fontana, rev. ed., 1989) remains the standard account but should be read in conjunction with **C. Haigh**, *English Reformations. Religion, politics and society under the Tudors* (Clarendon, 1993). **R. Swanson**, *Religion and Devotion in Europe 1215–1515* (CUP, 1995) puts the Reformation in its medieval context and **C. Lindberg**, *The European Reformations* (OUP, 1996) provides a sound account of the main reform movements in and beyond the sixteenth century. Three books by **K. Randell**, *Luther and the German Reformation* (Hodder & Stoughton, 1988), *Calvin and the Later Reformation* (Hodder & Stoughton, 1988) and *The Catholic and Counter Reformation* (Hodder & Stoughton, 1990) are useful starting points for AS/A Level students.

Biographies

There are many biographies of the leading reformers but few are suitable for AS/A Level students new to the subject. **R. Marius**, *Martin Luther: The Christian Between God and Death* (Harvard University Press, 1999) is the most recent account of Luther and is highly readable, while **H. A. Oberman**, *Luther, Man Between God and the Devil* (Yale UP, 1989) offers a compelling narrative. **A. E. McGrath**, *Luther's Theology of the Cross* (Blackwell, 1985) is a more demanding text. **H. J. Goertz**, *Thomas Müntzer: Apocalyptic Mystic and Revolutionary* (T and T Clark, 1993) is the most recent assessment of Müntzer and **D. F. Wright**, *Martin Bucer: Reforming Church and Community* (CUP, 1994) is an informed account of one of the more underrated figures of the Reformation period. The most readable accounts of Calvin are in **A. E. McGrath**, *A Life of John Calvin* (OUP, 1990), **W. G. Naphy**, *Calvin and the Consolidation of the Genevan Reformation* (March, 1994), and **G. R. Potter and M. Greengrass** (eds.), *John Calvin* (Arnold, 1983). **D. MacCulloch**'s *Thomas Cranmer: a Life* (Yale UP, 1996) provides a basic account of Cranmer.

Impact of the Reformation

J. Bossy, *Peace in the Post-Reformation* (CUP, 1998) is a short and stimulating essay on the consequences of the Reformation and **O. P. Grell** and **B. Scribner** (eds.), *Tolerance and Intolerance in the European Reformation* (CUP, 1996) survey violence and persecution in the sixteenth century. The main social effects are well served by **S. Ozment**, *When Fathers Ruled* (Harvard University Press, 1983), **R. Po-Chia Hsia**, *Social Discipline in the Reformation* (Routledge, 1989) and **M. Weisner**, *Women and Gender in Early Modern Europe* (CUP, 1993). **S. Michalski**, *The Reformation and the Visual Arts* (Routledge, 1993) is particularly good on painting and architecture during this period. Intellectual ideas are considered in **A. Goodman** and **A. Mackay** (eds.), *The Impact of Humanism on Western Europe* (CUP, 1990) and **A. E. McGrath**, *The Intellectual Origins of the European Reformation* (Blackwell, 1987). The role of printing and propaganda is dealt with in **M. U. Edwards**, *Printing, Propaganda and Martin Luther* (University of California Press, 1994) and **R. Scribner**, *For the Sake of Simple Folk: Popular Propaganda in the German Reformation* (CUP, 1981).

There are numerous national studies and the following recent works are accessible to most A Level students: **R. Po-Chia Hsia** (ed.), *The German People and the Reformation* (Ithaca, 1986), **R. Scribner**, *German Reformation* (Macmillan, 1986), **P. Blickle**, *Communal Reformation* (Humanities Press, 1993), **T. A. Brady**, *Turning Swiss. Cities and Empire, 1450–1550* (CUP, 1985), **M. Greengrass**, *The French Reformation* (Blackwell, 1987), **A. Duke**, *Reformation and Revolt in the Low Countries* (Hambledon, 1990), **B. Scribner**, **R. Porter** and **M. Teich** (eds.), *The Reformation in National Context* (CUP, 1994), and **K. Maag** (ed.), *The Reformation in Eastern and Central Europe* (St Andrews Studies in Reformation History, 1997). The English Reformation has been the subject of much research in recent years. **J. J. Scarisbrick**, *The Reformation and the English People* (Clarendon, 1982) first argued that it was a slow and conservative movement, and **E. Duffy**, *The Stripping of the Altars* (Yale University Press, 1992) takes a similar line in his highly entertaining study; **C. Marsh**, *Popular Religion in Sixteenth-Century England* (Macmillan, 1988) questions the revisionist and traditionalist interpretations, and **N. Tyacke** (ed.), *England's Long Reformation 1500–1800* (University College London, 1998) provides a series of very useful essays that set the sixteenth-century Reformation in a much wider context. **D. MacCulloch**, *Tudor Church Militant* (Allen Lane, 2000) is the most recent and highly acclaimed study of the Edwardian Reformation and **P. Collinson**, *The Culture of Puritanism, 1560–1700* (Basingstoke, 1996) is a far-ranging study by one of the leading authorities on English puritanism.

The impact of Calvinism is discussed in **M. Prestwich** (ed.), *International Calvinism, 1541–1715* (OUP, 1985), **A. Pettegree** (ed.), *The Early Reformation in Europe* (CUP, 1992), and **A. Duke**, **G. Lewis** and **A. Pettegree** (eds.), *Calvinism in Europe 1540–1620* (CUP, 1994). The following recent publications on the Catholic Reformation demonstrate the historical interest in this subject: **R. Bireley**, *The Counter Reformation* (Manchester University Press, 1998) offers an excellent assessment of the Catholic/Counter-Reformation debate; and **M. Mullett**, 'Counter-Reformation and Catholic Reformation revisited', *History Review* (2000) has also written a brief introduction to the subject which is ideal for AS students. **R. Po-Chia Hsia**, *The World of Catholic Renewal 1540–1770* (CUP, 1998) sets the impact of the Catholic revival in a geographically wider context. **J. O'Malley**, *The First Jesuits* (Cambridge, Mass., 1993) provides a sound account of the ideas and work of the Jesuits, and **H. Kamen**, *The Spanish Inquisition* (Phoenix Giant, 1998) has written a readable account of this much-maligned institution.

Index

Anabaptism 3–6, 42, 50, 52–6, 62–4
Anti-clericalism 17–20, 27, 39, 66
Anti-papalism 17, 27, 38, 68–70, 117
Augsburg 3, 15, 29–30, 33, 35, 37, 50, 53, 55, 96, 109–10, 117–18, 123

Basle 45, 50–2, 54, 88, 110–11, 122
Berne 50–2, 54, 58, 110
Bohemia 12, 26, 30, 106, 111, 116, 120, 123, 126
Bonner, Edmund 75, 77, 80–1, 86
Bucer, Martin 4, 21, 41–2, 47, 51, 56–7, 70, 73–4, 76–7, 110, 127, 131

Calvin, John 5, 21, 29, 42, 50, 56–62, 101, 110–12, 114–31
Catechisms 28, 38, 59–60, 67, 72, 95, 99, 101–2, 115–16, 129
Chantries 15–6, 27, 33, 67, 73, 75–9, 113, 122–3, 125–6
Charles V 33, 37, 74, 90–1, 96, 100, 109, 118, 123
Cologne 26, 28–30, 76, 101–2, 114
Confessions 60, 76, 93, 95, 101, 117, 124
Consistory 59–62, 115, 124, 128
Cranmer, Thomas 69–80
Cromwell, Thomas 69–73
Customs 13–17, 72, 75, 77, 84, 98, 115, 124–5

Dominicans 10, 20, 22, 32–4, 79, 89, 101, 114

Education 10, 29, 40, 42, 59, 62, 66, 80, 93–5, 106, 129–30
Edward VI 73–81, 122
Elizabeth I 70, 81–5, 110–11, 113, 119, 131
Erasmus, Desidirius 2, 19, 21–2, 27–9, 36, 46, 51, 57, 67, 75, 83, 101, 126

Florence 14, 16, 22, 88, 100, 125
Frederick the Wise 26, 33, 37

Gardiner, Stephen 72–3, 75, 77, 79–80
General council 8, 34–5, 89–91, 95, 97, 102, 105, 110
Geneva 56–62, 82–3, 111, 114, 119, 125

Henry VIII 15, 65–73, 116, 119, 122
Heresy 12–13, 16, 50, 61, 69, 71, 73, 78–80, 83, 99–102, 113, 119, 123, 126, 128
Humanism 20–3, 29, 41, 46, 51, 57, 60, 67, 94, 103
Hussites 12, 34, 111, 116

Iconoclasm 39–40, 72, 76, 111, 130
Index 98, 100–3, 114
Indulgences 3, 12–13, 15, 19, 21, 26–8, 31–3, 35, 46, 51, 56, 67, 97, 126
Inquisition 13, 89, 91, 98–105, 111, 113–15, 124
Italy 8–10, 12–13, 16–22, 27, 46, 56, 90–1, 94, 98, 100, 102–4, 106, 111, 117, 126, 130

Jesuits 5, 84, 92–5, 101–6, 114, 120, 127, 129–31

Karlstadt, Andreas 4, 34, 37, 53
Knox, John 77, 80, 119, 121

Latimer, Hugh 67–8, 71–2, 74–5, 77, 79–80
Leo X 7–8, 17, 19, 32–3, 89–90
Literacy 20–1, 115–16, 129–30
London 10, 13, 15–16, 18, 22, 66, 71, 74, 78–80, 83–4, 122–3, 127
Loyola, Ignatius 3, 92–5
Luther, Martin 3–6, 20–1, 25–44, 54–5, 57, 73–4, 93, 95–8, 100–1, 105, 109–12, 116–18, 120, 123–4, 126–32

Marburg 37, 47, 50, 110
Marriage 11, 39, 53–4, 77, 79, 82, 97, 127–9
Mary I 75, 78–81, 113
Melanchthon, Philip 4, 34, 47, 91, 110
Missionaries 62, 94–5, 105–6, 110
Monasteries 10, 31, 41, 47, 49–50, 58, 66, 70–1, 77, 79, 86, 89, 104, 111, 113, 119, 123
Moravia 53–5, 62, 111, 116, 122
Müntzer, Thomas 4, 53–4, 131
Music 29, 47, 83–4, 131
Mysticism 20, 32, 53–4, 93, 105

Netherlands 20, 25, 27, 52, 55, 62, 91–2, 100, 106, 110–11, 113, 115, 119–20, 123
Nuremberg 4, 27–30, 39–41, 73, 76, 117, 127

Orders, holy 10–11, 20, 89, 91–5, 98, 104–6, 113, 126–7

Painting 13, 21, 29, 38, 67, 101–2, 130–1
Papacy 3, 7–9, 12, 16–7, 27–8, 31–9, 46, 68–70, 78–9, 81–2, 84, 88–108, 114, 117, 125
Paul III 90–1, 93, 96, 100
Peasantry 30, 39–40, 50, 53–4, 105, 115, 118, 120, 122, 126
Persecution 53–4, 79–81, 111–3, 125–6
Philip II 79–80, 99–100, 104–5, 123
Pilgrimages 13–15, 28, 33, 57, 67, 71–2, 97–8, 115
Portugal 9 13, 94, 100, 106, 111, 117
Princes 9, 26–7, 39, 68, 90, 106, 117–18, 120–2, 126
Printing press 20, 28–9, 38, 40, 62, 66, 101–2, 122, 129–30
Purgatory 11–12, 15, 32–3, 71, 73, 76, 97

Rebellion 27, 50, 53, 71, 77–8, 84, 118–21
Rome 7–8, 15, 17, 19–20, 31–2, 89–93, 95, 98, 100, 102, 104, 106, 131

Sacraments 10–1, 20, 36–7, 47, 52, 57, 59, 67, 72, 80, 91, 93–4, 97, 104
Saints 12–15, 28, 33, 46, 66, 71–3, 80, 97–8, 103, 115, 125, 131
Saxony 15, 30–1, 33–4, 37, 39–40, 54, 71
Scotland 9, 75, 110–11, 117, 119
Spain 22, 89, 98–9, 101, 104–6, 111, 114, 117
Strasbourg 4, 16, 27–9, 40–2, 54–7, 74, 83, 117
Switzerland 18, 27, 45–62, 74, 110–11, 118, 122
Trent 5, 95–9, 101–2, 106, 110, 114, 125, 131

Universities 20–2, 31–2, 37, 45, 51, 54, 56, 62, 66–7, 69, 92, 98, 100–1, 130

Venice 14, 16, 92, 100, 102, 125
Vernacular 12, 40, 47, 53, 101, 129, 131
Visitations 1, 9, 40, 66, 75, 80, 97, 103, 114–15
Vulgate 13, 21, 29, 97, 103

Wittenberg 15, 21, 31, 34–5, 38–42, 49, 53, 67, 111, 127, 129,
Women 10, 20, 53, 73, 80, 92, 99, 104, 123, 129

Zurich 46–52, 54, 74, 84, 122
Zwingli, Ulrich 4, 21, 29, 37, 41–2, 45–51, 54, 57, 62, 73–5, 77, 110–2, 118, 124, 126, 131